W9-CKQ-530

CONTENTS

INTRODUCTION

The Battle of the Bulge in December 1944–January 1945 was the last great clash of armor in the West in World War II. In a desperate gamble to reverse Germany's declining fortunes, Hitler threw away his last panzer reserves in a futile effort to cripple the inexorable Allied advance. The tank fighting in the Ardennes provides an intriguing subject for Osprey's Duel series. On the face of it, the contest between Sherman and Panther seems preordained in the Panther's favor. On paper, the Panther was more than a match for the Sherman, with a much more powerful gun and much better frontal armor. Yet paper statistics do not decide the outcome of battles, and they have less effect on combat than is often assumed. Technical superiority does not necessarily translate into tactical success on the battlefield. Other factors – the quality and training of soldiers, the tactics they employ, the conditions of the battlefield – usually have a far greater impact than the technological balance alone. The aim of this book is to examine the battle from this perspective, pitting the US Army's M4A3 (76mm) medium tank against the German Panther Ausf. G medium tank.

Most popular accounts focus on the technological balance between tanks as the basis for comparing their prospects in battle. Yet operational research in World War II suggests otherwise. The results of these studies are not well known outside professional military circles, but they offer a sharply different view of tank-versus-tank combat in World War II. These studies suggest that the primary factor in deciding victor and vanquished in tank combat was not the technological balance, but who spotted the enemy tank first, who engaged first, and who hit first.

Many assessments of World War II tanks are based on the false notion that tank-versus-tank combat was the predominant mission of tank units in World War II. This was certainly not the case of either German or American tank units in northwest

PANTHER VS SHERMAN

Battle of the Bulge 1944

STEVEN J ZALOGA

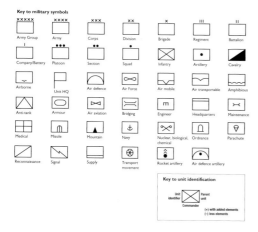

Key to military symbols

Army Group	Army	Corps	Division	Brigade	Regiment	Battalion
Company/Battery	Platoon	Section	Squad	Infantry	Artillery	Cavalry
Airborne	Unit HQ	Air defence	Air Force	Air mobile	Air transportable	Amphibious
Anti-tank	Armour	Air aviation	Bridging	Engineer	Headquarters	Maintenance
Medical	Missile	Mountain	Navy	Nuclear, biological, chemical	Ordnance	Parachute
Reconnaissance	Signal	Supply	Transport movement	Rocket artillery	Air defence artillery	

Key to unit identification

Unit identifier — Parent unit
Commander
(+) with added elements
(−) less elements

First published in Great Britain in 2008 by Osprey Publishing,
Midland House, West Way, Botley, Oxford OX2 0PH, UK
443 Park Avenue South, New York, NY 10016, USA

E-mail: info@ospreypublishing.com

A CIP catalogue record for this book is available from the British Library

ISBN: 978 1 84603 292 9

Page layouts by Myriam Bell Design, France
Digital artwork by Jim Laurier
Battlescene by Howard Gerrard
Index by Glyn Sutcliffe
Typeset in Adobe Garamond and ITC Conduit
The Map Studio and the Peter Bull Art Studio
Originated by PDQ Digital Media Solutions
Printed in China through Bookbuilders

09 10 11 12 13   11 10 9 8 7 6 5 4 3 2

FOR A CATALOGUE OF ALL BOOKS PUBLISHED BY OSPREY MILITARY
AND AVIATION PLEASE CONTACT:

NORTH AMERICA

Osprey Direct, c/o Random House Distribution Center,
400 Hahn Road, Westminster, MD 21157, USA
E-mail: uscustomerservice@ospreypublishing.com

ALL OTHER REGIONS

Osprey Direct, The Book Service Ltd, Distribution Centre, Colchester Road,
Frating Green, Colchester, Essex, CO7 7DW
E-mail: customerservice@ospreypublishing.com

www.ospreypublishing.com

Osprey Publishing is supporting the Woodland Trust, the UK's leading woodland
conservation charity, by funding the dedication of trees.

Editor's note

For ease of comparison please refer to the
following conversion table:

1 mile = 1.6km

1lb = 0.45kg

1yd = 0.9m

1ft = 0.3m

1in. = 2.54cm/25.4mm

1gal = 4.5 liters

1 ton (US) = 0.9 tonnes

Author's note

The author would especially like to thank David Fletcher
of the Tank Museum, Bovington, for his help with
documents used in this book and Bill Auerbach for help
with photos.

Europe in 1944–45. Tanks were the spearhead of combined arms operations, always used in conjunction with infantry to overcome enemy defenses and to exploit breakthroughs by rapid advance. More often than not, these missions involved actions against enemy infantry. Encounters with enemy tanks, while not rare, were not a daily occurrence except in major campaigns. Tank-versus-tank fighting was the most dramatic form of tank combat in World War II but neither the most common nor the most important.

An M4A3 (76mm) of Co. C, 774th Tank Battalion, passes by a knocked-out Panther tank near Bovigny on January 17, 1945, while supporting the 83rd Division during the drive to seal the Bulge. (NARA)

The Panther tank had formidable armament and superior armor protection to the Sherman, yet ultimately its performance in the Ardennes operation was disappointing. In the hands of an experienced crew, the Panther was clearly superior to the Sherman. The victories of the occasional panzer ace could not overcome the lackluster performance of the majority of the crews. Too many of the Wehrmacht crews in the winter of 1944–45 were inexperienced with minimal training. In combination with the Panther's technical weaknesses – its poor powertrain durability, lack of fuel, and lack of spare parts – the declining quality of German tank crews resulted more frequent breakdowns which many times resulted in the loss of the tank when it could not be recovered or repaired.

Tank warfare in World War II depended upon mass as well as technical quality. The Sherman tank prevailed in the Battle of the Bulge because it was more reliable and more numerous than the Panther. The Sherman was used not only by the armored divisions, but in support of the infantry divisions as well. While it might not be equal in a duel with a Panther, the Sherman performed well enough in its more common battlefield missions.

CHRONOLOGY

1941
February — Development of Sherman begins.

December — Development of Panther begins.

1942
February — Production of M4A1 (75mm) begins.

June — Production of M4A3 (75mm) begins.

November — Production of Panther Ausf. D begins.

1943
June — Development of M4 with T23 (76mm) turret begins.

August — Production of Panther Ausf. A begins.

This was one of five Panthers of the first company of SS-Panzer Regt. 12 that fought their way into Krinkelt around 0730hrs on December 18. Four were knocked out by bazooka teams and antitank guns, and this vehicle escaped down the Büllingen road where it was knocked out by an M10 3-in. gun motor carriage (GMC) of the 644th Tank Destroyer Battalion around 1100hrs. It had 11 bazooka hits, several 57mm hits, and three 3-in. impacts in the rear, a testament to the Panther's formidable protection. (NARA)

September — Production of Panther Ausf. D ends.

December — Production of M4A1 (75mm) ends.

1944
January — Production of M4A1 (76mm) begins.

March — Production of Panther Ausf. G begins.

April — Production of M4A3 (76mm) begins. First 76mm Shermans arrive in European Theater of Operations.

July — Production of Panther Ausf. A ends.

August — Production of M4A3E8 (76mm) begins.

October 11 — First draft of Ardennes plan, codenamed *Wacht am Rhein*, submitted to Hitler.

October 22 — Senior German commanders are briefed on the Ardennes plan.

November	First German units begin moving into the Eifel for the offensive at the beginning of the month.
December	Production of M4A3, M4A3E8 (76mm) ends.
December 16	X-Day, start of German Ardennes offensive begins with opening barrages against forward US positions in Ardennes.
December 25	Delivery of first M4A3E8 (76mm) to deployed unit in ETO.

1945

February	Production of M4A3 (75mm) ends.
April	Production of Panther Ausf G ends.

ABOVE This particular Panther Ausf. G of SS-Pz.Rgt. 2 was one of several lost in the fighting at Manhay on the road from Trois Ponts. It is being inspected by US troops in early January after the town was retaken. (NARA)

BELOW The crew of an M4A3 (76mm), Co. A, 774th Tank Battalion is seen here whitewashing their tank in Joubieval on January 17, 1945, while supporting the 83rd Division in counterattacks against the remnants of the Bulge.

DESIGN AND DEVELOPMENT

THE PANTHER TANK

The Panther tank had been developed in response to the tank crisis that befell the Wehrmacht during the invasion of Russia in June 1941. Further details of the Panther's early development are covered in another book in the Duel series, *Panther vs T-34, Ukraine 1943*.

The Panther represented a significant shift in tank design philosophy, fostered in large measure by Germany's changing military fortunes. Until 1942, German medium tanks had been similar in weight and size to their adversaries, and often lighter. The lighter armor and firepower of the panzers was not deemed tactically significant as the primary mission of the panzer divisions was offensive, to exploit breakthroughs won by the infantry, using the panzers' speed and mobility. Even if not ideally suited for tank-versus-tank combat, the PzKpfw III and PzKpfw IV were durable, reliable machines suitable for mobile operations. Germany's declining military prospects in 1942 shifted the emphasis away from an offensive orientation that put a premium on mobility and durability toward a more defensive orientation that depended upon overmatching Soviet tanks in firepower and protection. The focus was a new long-range 75mm gun to attrite the numerically superior enemy tank force in the flat plains of Russia. Although the original design focused on the gun, the Panther gradually crept up in weight as more armor was added: from 22 tonnes in the original 1941 designs to about 40 tonnes by the time the design entered production. Declining supplies of critical steel alloys forced the plants to rely on armor steel with a high carbon content, requiring complex interlocking plates due to welding issues. In the haste to put the design into production, insufficient attention was paid to the impact of the weight increases on the power train, and the Panther would be plagued by durability problems because its engine and final drives were better suited to the original, lighter proposals. By any other army's definition, the Panther was a heavy tank. Although originally intended to replace the existing PzKpfw III and PzKpfw IV medium tanks, its cost and complexity limited the scale of its production. By 1944, the Wehrmacht was saddled with a mixed fleet of Panthers and PzKpfw IV tanks instead of an integrated fleet, burdening the army with both logistics and training difficulties.

The Panther design reflected the German industry's penchant for craftsmanship that favored optimal design over mass production considerations. For example, advanced torsion bar suspension was chosen over Daimler-Benz's more traditional leaf spring design and was compromised by the use of complicated interleaved road wheels. While offering a more comfortable ride cross-country, it provided no tactical advantage, yet was more expensive to manufacture and to maintain in the field. The Panther was a clear example of the engineering adage that "perfection is the enemy of excellence." The extravagance of the Panther's design inevitably meant that it would fight outnumbered.

The development of the Panther was part of a larger effort by the Wehrmacht to strengthen the panzer force due to the demands of the vast Russian front. In September 1942, Hitler demanded that AFV (armored fighting vehicle) production reach 1,400 vehicles per month by spring 1944, including 600 Panthers. The Adolf Hitler Panzer Program put forward by Albert Speer's Ministry of Armaments and War Production in January 1943 was only 1,200 AFVs per month, and that goal could not be met before the critical summer 1944 campaign. Infuriated, Hitler summoned Speer for a meeting at which he increased the objective to 1,500–2,000 AFVs per month, comparable to Soviet or American production. Although Hitler's goals would never

The Panther developed a fearsome reputation among US tankers after initial encounters in mid-July with the Panzer Lehr Division. But the combat effectiveness of the Panther regiments against the US Army was low during most of the summer due to tactical misuse. This Panther Ausf. A was lost during the fighting around Falaise in early August 1944. (NARA)

By the time of the Ardennes fighting, the Panther regiments had been reequipped with the new Panther Ausf. G, which featured an improved hull. This is an example from the September 1944 production at MAN in Nuremberg using steel-rimmed road wheels, an uncommon variant of the series. (NARA)

be met, the new priority given to tank production doubled resources so that AFV production went from 3.8 percent of the armaments production at the beginning of 1942 to 7.9 percent by the end of 1943, with AFV production doubling from 6,180 in 1942 to 12,013 in 1943.

Although the Panther had the potential to emerge as one of the great tanks of World War II, the first version, which debuted at Kursk in summer 1943, suffered appallingly poor reliability. On average, only one-quarter of the Panther Ausf. D tanks deployed in the panzer regiments in 1943 were operational at any given time. While technical difficulties are not unusual in any new weapon system, the Panther was worse than average. This situation gradually improved through the course of 1943 as specific shortcomings were rectified. The Panther's operational rate rose from an appalling 16 percent at the end of July 1943 to the merely wretched rate of 37 percent by December 1943.

PANTHER SIDE-VIEW

8.6m

An improved version, confusingly called the Panther Ausf. A, entered production in August 1943. This version standardized improvements that had been gradually introduced into the Panther Ausf. D and included an improved turret with a new commander's cupola. Additional changes continued to be incorporated into the design through 1943 and into 1944. These improvements began to have an effect on the availability rate of the tanks deployed on the Eastern Front, going from 37 percent in February to 50 percent in April and 78 percent by the end of

PANTHER SPECIFICATIONS

Panther Ausf. G, II./SS-Pz.Rgt. 1, Kampfgruppe Peiper, La Gleize, Belgium, December 1944

General
Crew: 5 (commander, gunner, loader, driver, radioman)
Combat weight: 44.8 metric tons
Power-to-weight ratio: 15.5hp/T
Overall length: 8.6m
Width: 3.4m
Height: 2.9m

Motive power
Engine: Maybach HL 230 P 30 12-cylinder; 700hp at 3,000rpm
Transmission: AK 7-200; seven forward, one reverse

Fuel capacity: 720 liters

Performance
Max. speed (road): 55km/h
Max. speed (cross-country): 30km/h
Range: 70–130km
Fuel consumption: 2.8 to 7 liters per km (road/cross-country)
Ground pressure: 0.88 bar

Armament
Main armament: 7.5cm KwK L/70 with coaxial 7.62mm LMG
Secondary armament: two MG 34 LMG
Main gun Ammunition: 82 rounds 7.5cm, 4,200 rounds 7.92mm
Armor: 100mm (turret mantlet); 45mm (turret side); 80mm (glacis); 40mm (hull side)

PANTHER FRONT VIEW

3.4m

PANTHER REAR VIEW

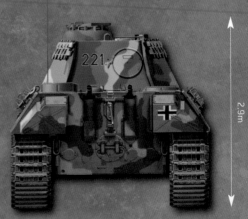

2.9m

The oddest Panthers fielded in the Ardennes were five that were converted to look like US M10 tank destroyers for use by Skorzeny's Panzer Brigade 150. This was the ersatz M10 of Lt Gerstenschlager, abandoned at the attack on Malmedy on December 21 near the Café du Rocher de Falize. (NARA)

May 1944. Although it debuted in the West at Anzio in February 1944, the Panther saw little combat during the counteroffensive against the Anzio beachhead. Due to the muddy ground conditions, the corps commander ordered the Panther battalion held in reserve, and the Panther did not see extensive combat in Italy until May 1944.

The German tank industry was spared from major strategic bomber attacks through 1943, and none of the Panther tank plants were significantly bombed until summer 1944. In spite of the lack of attacks, Panther production never reached the intended goal of 600 per month, peaking in July 1944 at 379 tanks. Due to a focus on other targets such as German fighter plants, the Allies attempted to locate a bottleneck in German tank production rather than attack each plant individually. Recognizing that Panthers and Tigers were powered by Maybach engines, the Maybach plant was struck by the RAF on the night of April 27/28, 1944, which essentially stopped production for five months through September 1944. This would have halted Panther production but for Speer's prescient decision to disperse production, and the second source, the Auto-Union plant at Siegmar, came online in May 1944, narrowly averting a disaster in the panzer industry.

By spring 1944, greater attention was being applied to all German armament programs to increase production by simplifying designs. In the case of the Panther, this involved the adoption of some features from the aborted Panther 2 design to the new Panther Ausf. G such as the simplified side armor plate design, which also increased side armor protection from 40 to 50mm. Many small changes were also introduced, including redesigned hull crew hatches, a new traversable driver's periscope mounting, and an improved power train cooling system. Production of the Panther Ausf. G began in March 1944, and this type began to appear on the Western Front in late summer 1944. This would be the standard Panther production type until the end of the war and the principal version in the Battle of the Bulge.

Although Panther production continued to increase until July 1944, it began to suffer from the consequences of the Allied bombing program and the fortunes of war, losing access to metal alloys critical in steel production. In February 1944, the Wehrmacht lost control of the Soviet manganese mines at Nikopol and Krivoy Rog in Ukraine. Access to molybdenum was cut off by Allied bomber attacks on the Knaben mine in Norway as well the end of supplies from Finland and Japan. As a result, the molybdenum content in thick armor plate fell from a high of about 0.55 percent in 1943 to 0.25 percent in mid-1944 to none at all in 1945, leading to declining shock properties in the Panther's armor. In combination with declining industrial quality control in the quenching process, the Panther's armor, though still very hard, became increasingly brittle, leading to fracturing and decreased impact resistance. By some estimates, as much as half of the Panther armor was flawed, losing about 10 to 20 percent of its effectiveness. Quality control was further undermined by the extensive use of foreign forced labor in the panzer plants, and there is some evidence from recent museum restorations of deliberate sabotage of Panther fuel and lubrication lines.

In August 1944, the RAF and USAAF began a systematic air campaign against the German tank and vehicle industry. The main Panther plant, MAN at Nüremberg, was hit hard on September 10, 1944, costing the Wehrmacht the equivalent of over four months production, or about 645 tanks. Daimler-Benz was hit as well, but the second most important plant, the MNH (Maschinenfabrik Niedersachsen) in Hanover, was ignored until March 1945. Aside from a very successful campaign against the Henschel King Tiger plant in Kassel, the Allies were unhappy with the results of the raids, and the attacks petered out in October, only to be resumed in the wake of the Battle of the Bulge. While they may not have had the immediate results expected by Allied bomber chiefs, they had insidious effects on the panzer force. Speer

Virtually all the Panthers that saw combat in the Ardennes were newly manufactured from September to November production runs. This is a Panther Ausf. G of the II./Pz.Rgt. 9, 9th Panzer Division being inspected by GIs of the 83rd Division in late December lost during the attempts to rescue the trapped 2nd Panzer Division beyond Bastogne. (NARA)

13

was able to keep panzer production at adequate levels through the end of 1944 by shifting plant resources away from other products, such as trucks, and focusing on tanks. More critically, the Panther plants dramatically cut production of spare parts, which in 1943 had constituted as much as 25 to 30 percent of the tank contracts. By summer 1944, only about 15 percent of Maybach engines were put aside as spares, and by autumn 1944, this had been halved to only about 8 percent. This hidden cost of the air campaign would have dire consequences for the Panther regiments during the Battle of the Bulge due to the confluence of the continuing unreliability of some key Panther components such as final drives and the growing decline in spare parts. When replacement Panthers were sent to the Ardennes in December 1944, they were cannibalized for parts rather than being issued, in order to repair the numerous broken down Panthers already with frontline units.

The most critical loss of resources occurred in summer 1944 with the end of oil supplies from Romania, Germany's main source of fuel. The strict rationing of fuel limited driver training, and as will be noted below, the Panther regiments deployed to the Ardennes depended on new panzer crewmen. The Panther was a complicated tank to drive, and more importantly, the lack of adequate driver training combined with the power train problems led to frequent breakdowns. This contributed to poor operational readiness in the units and sometimes led to the abandonment of the Panthers in combat when they could not be quickly repaired or retrieved.

In spite of its impressive technical qualities, the combat performance of the Panther battalions against the US Army in summer 1944 was almost universally poor. Its combat debut with the Panzer Lehr Division during the counterattack at La Desert

One of the improvements on some Pather Ausf. G was the use of a new cast gun mantlet with a "chin" at the bottom to prevent tank shells from ricocheting into the thin roof armor above the driver. This Panther Ausf. G of the 1st SS-Panzer Divison was knocked out in the fighting near the Baugnez crossroads and has suffered a catastrophic ammunition fire, evident from the blown-out sponson floor sitting on the tracks. (NARA)

in mid-July was a fiasco with many tanks lost; the divisional commander complained about its clumsy performance in the close terrain of the French hedgerows. Operation *Lüttich*, the August counteroffensive that attempted to cut off Patton's Third Army by a drive to Avranches, was another fiasco, due to tactical mistakes and not any technical problems with the Panthers. The most embarrassing performance of the Panther was in September when Hitler shifted several newly formed panzer brigades to Lorraine to combat Patton's rapid advance towards Frankfurt. The poor training of new Panther crews led to a series of costly defeats culminating in the swirling tank melees at Arracourt, the largest tank-versus-tank battle fought by the US Army until the Battle of the Bulge and a resounding flop for the Panther.[1]

THE M4A3 (76MM) SHERMAN

The M4A3 (76mm) represented the second generation of the Sherman tank family.[2] The design of the first generation of the Sherman tank began in spring 1941, to replace the interim M3 Lee/Grant medium tank. Production started in February 1942, and the many subvariants of the Sherman were distinguished mainly by engine

The combat debut of the 76mm Sherman was Operation *Cobra* on July 24, 1944, when the US Army began the Normandy breakout. Both 2nd and 3rd Armored Divisions were equipped with over 50 of this new type for the operation, and many of these tanks were still in service at the time of the Ardennes fighting. (NARA)

---

1   See Osprey Campaign 75, *Lorraine 1944, Patton vs Manteuffel.*
2   For more details on the development of the 76mm Sherman, see Osprey New Vanguard 73, *M4 (76mm) Sherman Medium Tank 1943–65.*

The crew of an M4A1 (76mm) of the 2nd Armored Division repair the track in a wooded area near Amonines, Belgium, in early January 1945 in the midst of a snow storm. This tank was probably a Normandy veteran, as most replacement 76mm Shermans were the M4A3 type. (NARA)

types: the welded hull M4 and cast hull M4A1 with a Continental radial aircraft engine, the M4A2 with twin truck diesels, the M4A3 with a Ford GAA in-line gasoline aircraft engine, and the M4A4 with a conglomeration of bus engines in a star pattern. Tank production was given less priority than aircraft production, and so the Sherman had to make do with whatever engines were available instead of relying on a single type. Although "Sherman" was a British name for the M4 family and not used by the US Army in World War II, it will be used here for convenience.

The Sherman was principally intended for use by the new armored divisions. The primary mission of the armored divisions was the old cavalry role of exploitation of the breakthrough after the penetration had been won by the infantry. As such, due to its offensive orientation, the balance of the design placed greater emphasis on mobility and firepower than on armor. The US Army's other principal armored units, the separate tank battalions, would have favored a design with better armored protection, due to their mission of infantry support, but the head of the Army Ground Forces (AGF), Gen Lesley McNair, favored ruthless standardization of tank designs, realizing that the US Army would be fighting its battles thousands of miles from the tank plants in Detroit and could ill afford logistical complications. McNair defined the two primary requirements of US tank design as battle worthiness and battle need. Battle worthiness demanded sufficient ruggedness and reliability to withstand the rigors of combat service without imposing excessive maintenance. This policy tended to favor a more conservative approach to tank design once a satisfactory type such as the Sherman was already in service. Battle need meant that acquisition was not encouraged unless combat experience had demonstrated both the need for the new equipment and that local theater commanders specifically demanded the new equipment. While this might seem reasonable on the surface, this type of reactive policy overlooked the "tyranny of time" – the long delay between the point when the need was articulated by field commanders to the months or years it took to develop and field new equipment. McNair's twin policies lay at the heart of the Sherman's virtues and vices.

When introduced into combat at El Alamein in autumn 1942, the Sherman was widely praised as the best Allied tank in the field, with an excellent blend of firepower, armor, and mobility. Its combat debut in Tunisia with the US Army was not auspicious, but the defeat of US tank battalions in the Kasserine Pass battles was rightly attributed to poor Allied leadership, inexperienced US units, and immature tactical doctrine. In the wake of the fighting in Tunisia and the later operation on Sicily, a number of incremental improvements were recommended for the Sherman, and a "Quick-Fix" program was initiated in spring 1943 to retrofit Shermans in the European Theater of Operations (ETO) with these features. The US Army's tank battalions in the ETO in summer 1944 were equipped with the M4 and M4A1 until some of the new second-generation M4A3 tanks began appearing later in the year.

Even though there was no indication from the theater commanders that a better armed version of the Sherman was needed, the Ordnance Department inevitably tinkered with armament improvements. The M1 76mm gun was a refined version of the 3-in. gun on the M10 tank destroyer, better suited for fitting inside a small tank turret. While this weapon did fit in the existing Sherman tank turret, the fit was tight, and the long barrel threw off the turret balance, making it difficult to traverse. Since there was no strong demand for much better antitank performance at the time, Ordnance lopped off 15in. from the barrel, decreasing its antiarmor penetration by about 10 percent rather than rebalance the turret with counterweights. In contrast to the American complacency, the British Army had seen a steady escalation in tank firepower and armor since the start of the war, progressing from the 2-pdr (40mm) of 1939 to the 6-pdr (57mm) of 1941 to the 75mm in 1942. The British were already working on their own new 76mm gun, better known as the 17-pdr. In contrast to the American indifference for a new tank gun, the British tankers demanded a high-performance tank killer. The best approach to improve the penetrating power of an antitank projectile was to increase the amount of propellant in the round and to

The most common version of the 76mm Sherman was the M4A3 (76mm), and some units arriving in the ETO in autumn 1944 were completely equipped with this type, such as the 9th Armored Division. This M4A3 (76) of Co. C, 19th Tank Battalion, Task Force Collins, CCA, 9th Armored Division is seen moving forward on December 27, 1944, as part of the effort to open the road from Neufchateau to Bastogne. (NARA)

lengthen the barrel so that the propellant had more time to accelerate the projectile down the tube. The 17-pdr barrel was not much longer than the M1 76mm gun, 55cal versus 52cal, but the British round contained almost 9lb of propellant compared to 3.6lb in the US round. The German Panther used a slightly different approach, with only 8.1lb of propellant but with a much longer 70cal barrel. As a result, the American gun could penetrate about 115mm of armor at 500m, but the British and German guns could punch through 165mm. US tank doctrine did not anticipate tank-versus-tank fighting to be the primary mission of its armored force, and combat experience to date had shown that well over three-fourths of the tank ammunition expended was high explosive, not armor piercing.

By summer 1943, the US Army was beginning to get their first impressions of the technical details of the Panther. The Red Army captured several Panthers during the battle of Kursk, so British and American liaison officers in Moscow had an opportunity to see and photograph one as well as receive basic technical details, including armor layout. This did not create much of a stir in the US Army due to a serious misconception about the Panther's role. Allied intelligence at first viewed the Panther as simply another heavy tank like the Tiger that would be issued on a small scale to corps-level independent tank battalions as was the case at Kursk. The Allies had faced the Tiger in Tunisia, Sicily, and Italy, recognizing it as a formidable adversary, but they discounted it from tank policy since it was so rarely encountered. It was not until late spring 1944, shortly before D-Day, that Allied intelligence began to appreciate that the Wehrmacht intended to deploy the Panther as a standard medium tank in the panzer divisions. As a result, the Panther threat began to be realized too late to have an impact on US Army decisions for its 1944 tank program. The US Army believed that their 76mm gun could penetrate the Panther mantlet at 400m and the Tiger mantlet at 200m, but this would prove to be wrong.

The US Army gave little serious consideration to adopting the British 17-pdr as an alternative to the new 76mm M1A1 gun. US Army Ordnance officers who witnessed

SHERMAN SIDE-VIEW

COME IN

U.S.A.
30114457 S

24.2ft

test firings in the UK in autumn 1943 were flabbergasted by the enormous muzzle blast and shocked by flashbacks emanating from the breech, which suggested design immaturity. The first demonstrations of 17-pdrs mounted in Sherman turrets did not take place until December 1943, after the US Army's 1944 tank program had already been established. Most importantly, there was no strong pressure from armor officers in the ETO for an improved antitank weapon, as there was no widespread recognition

SHERMAN SPECIFICATIONS

M4A3 (76mm), Co. C, 22nd Tank Battalion, 11th Armored Division, Bastogne area, January 1945

General
Crew: 5 (commander, gunner, loader, driver, co-driver)
Combat weight: 36 tons
Power-to-weight ratio: 11.3hp/T
Overall length: 24.2ft
Width: 8.9ft
Height: 11.2ft

Motive power
Engine: Ford GAA 8-cylinder; 500hp at 2600rpm
Transmission: Syncromesh with five forward, one reverse speed with two-plate dry disc clutch

Fuel capacity: 172gal Max. speed (road): 24mph Max. speed (cross-country): 16mph

Performance
Range: 100mi
Fuel consumption: 1.7gal per mile
Ground pressure: 14.5psi (12.3psi with extended end connectors)

Armament
Main armament: M1A1 76mm gun in M62 combination mount with coaxial .30cal machine gun
Secondary armament: .50cal. Browning M2 HB HMG on turret and .30 cal. Browning LMG in hull
Main gun Ammunition: 71 rounds 76mm ammunition
Armor: 89mm (gun mantlet); 63mm (turret side); 63–108mm (hull front); 38mm (hull side)

SHERMAN FRONT VIEW

8.9ft

SHERMAN REAR VIEW

11.2ft

of the shortcomings of the 76mm gun against Panther armor. In the absence of a strong "battle need," production of a limited number of the available 76mm M1A1 gun seemed the prudent course.

The 1944 US Army tank program began limited 76mm Sherman production on the M4A1 chassis in January 1944, followed by the M4A3 chassis, which had been selected in 1943 as the favored chassis for future US Army requirements due to its superior automotive performance. The adoption of the 76mm gun coincided with a significant redesign of the Sherman hull to incorporate "wet" ammunition stowage, representing a second generation of Shermans. The fighting in Tunisia and Italy had demonstrated the vulnerability of Shermans to ammunition fires. The wet stowage program moved the ammunition out of the vulnerable sponsons down into the floor, introduced armored ammunition bins to reduce the likelihood of fragments penetrating the highly flammable propellant cases, and encased the ammunition stowage tubes in liquid to reduce the chances of hot fragments igniting the propellant should they penetrate the new bins. The 1944 tank program planned to build the second-generation Sherman in a mix of 75mm and 76mm types that could be altered during the year should the need arise for more of the new 76mm gun versions.

The first batch of 130 M4A1 (76mm) were shipped to England in April 1944. They were greeted with complete disdain by the US tank commanders who disliked the inferior high-explosive projectile, which contained only about half the high explosive of the round for the 75mm gun. Patton categorically refused to accept them for his units. The original version of the M1A1 76mm gun lacked a muzzle brake, as fitted to the German Panther and British Firefly, so it kicked up more dust in front of the tank when firing, obscuring the target at precisely the moment that confirmation was needed as to whether the first round had hit or not. As a result, the 130 M4A1 (76mm) guns were not issued to any units in Britain prior to D-Day and were orphaned to an ordnance depot.

The Sherman's availability in summer 1944 was a complete contrast to the Panther experience. The US Army had imposed tough requirements on tank reliability, and the Sherman was vigorously tested at Aberdeen Proving Ground to ensure its durability. Simplification and standardization had been incorporated into the design from the outset to permit mass production, since the Sherman was being delivered not only to the US Army, but the British, Soviet, and French armies as well. Sherman units in the field regularly maintained availability rates of 90 percent or better, and the Sherman was much simpler to maintain and repair than the Panther, with an ample spares reserve as well. Sherman production in 1943 had been 21,250 compared to only 1,830 Panthers. The difference between the German and American tank production programs was not based so much on tank philosophy but rather on the strategic orientation of their armies. When the Wehrmacht had staged its blitzkrieg campaigns in the early war years, it had favored lighter, cheaper, and more reliable tanks such as the Sherman. But since Germany had been forced onto the strategic defensive since 1943, it had shifted its requirements toward firepower and protection and away from mass, durability, and operational mobility.

TECHNICAL SPECIFICATIONS

PROTECTION

The Panther had significantly better armor protection than the Sherman. The hull glacis armor of the Panther Ausf. G was 80mm of rolled homogenous armor (RHA) at an angle of 55 degrees from the vertical. This angle gave the Panther roughly the equivalent of 145mm of armor in direct frontal attack. The equivalent thickness is due to the geometric effect of the slope, although some deflection of shot could occur depending on the projectile.[3] The Panther's turret front was protected by a rounded, cast mantlet, 100mm thick. This proved to be the Achilles heel of the Panther in frontal combat, as Allied tankers found that if their rounds hit the lower portion of the mantlet, the rounds often ricocheted downward through the thin hull roof armor into the ammo racks immediately below. This led to the introduction of new mantlet design in September 1944 featuring a thickened "chin" to avoid this problem, although tanks continued to be manufactured with the older mantlet for some months. The glacis armor of the Panther was essentially invulnerable to the 76mm gun on the M4A3 (76mm) when the gun fired the normal M62 armor-piercing ammunition that could only penetrate 116mm of RHA at 500 meters; lucky hits could penetrate the mantlet at close range.

---

3   For readers interested in more details on tank gun ballistics and armor performance, the author recommends more specialized studies such as Lorrin Bird and Robert Livingstone's, *World War II Ballistics: Armor and Gunnery*, Overmatch, 2001.

Although the Panther had formidable armor protection from the front, its side protection was much weaker, with 45mm at 25 degrees on the turret side and 50mm at 30 degrees on the upper hull side, equivalent to about 50mm and 60mm respectively, depending on the angle of attack. The Panther could be penetrated from the side by the M4A3 (76mm) at typical combat ranges. The stowage of 52 rounds of ammunition in the side sponsons made this area the most vulnerable point on the Panther since penetration here usually led to catastrophic ammunition fires. The Panther had mediocre overhead protection, especially on the engine deck. There were a large number of openings for engine air intake and cooling that made the engine compartment vulnerable to overhead artillery airbursts and to heavy machine gun fire from strafing aircraft.

The M4A3 (76mm) had a front glacis plate 63mm thick at 47 degrees and a cast turret mantlet 91mm thick. Both areas were vulnerable to the Panther gun at standard combat ranges. The upper hull sides were 38mm vertical and were also vulnerable to the Panther's gun at standard ranges. In contrast to the earlier versions of the Sherman, which stowed ammunition in the sponson, the introduction of the wet stowage feature on the 76mm Shermans was accompanied by the transfer of the ammunition into protected bins on the floor of the tank, which greatly reduced the probability of them being hit and also reduced the probability that the ammunition would be ignited by a penetration elsewhere in the tank by bits of projectile or debris. An army study in 1945 concluded that only 10–15 percent of the wet stowage Shermans burned when penetrated compared to 60–80 percent of the older dry stowage Shermans.

The Sherman had a reputation as a fire trap allegedly due to the propensity of its gasoline to burn. This perception is mistaken from two aspects: the Panther and most German tanks also used gasoline for fuel, and the primary cause of catastrophic tank

The Panther offered formidable protection against the 76mm, as seen in this test conducted on a captured early production Ausf. G at Saverne, France, in February 1945 by the US Seventh Army. Of the eight hits on the tank, five failed to penetrate. One penetrated the mantlet, one bounced off the bottom of the mantlet into the hull roof, and one cracked the glacis armor at the joint with the lower bow plate. (NARA)

fires was not fuel but ammunition propellant. Most World War II tanks had large amounts of ammunition stowed in the forward hull, and it was far more likely that this would be hit during fighting than the rear fuel cells. Once ignited, ammunition propellant fires were impossible to stop, and if the fires spread to neighboring ammunition, the results were generally disastrous. Both the Panther and Sherman had fire-extinguishing systems to deal with gasoline fires, though their effectiveness depended very much on the circumstances of the fires. The Sherman was no more susceptible to fire due to its fuel than the Panther, but it was more vulnerable to fire simply because it was more vulnerable to being penetrated in combat. The Panther had a poor reputation regarding fire safety among German tank crews due to the fire hazard of the hydraulic fluid used in the transmission, fuel leaks in the complicated fuel cell linkage, and fires caused by engine back blast, but its excellent armor reduced the likelihood that it would be penetrated in tank combat.

The Panther's side armor remained vulnerable to a wide range of weapons. This Panther Ausf. G, of the 9th SS-Panzer Division, was knocked out by a 57mm antitank gun during the fighting for Langlir, to the northeast of Houfallize, on January 13, 1945. The penetration can be seen on the turret rear at the bottom of the tactical number 121. In the hands of brave crews, the infantry's obsolete 57mm antitank gun remained a major hazard to Panthers in the Ardennes. (NARA)

FIREPOWER

The Panther had superior firepower to the M4A3 (76mm) in tank-versus-tank combat. The standard antitank ammunition for its 7.5cm KwK 42 gun was the Pzgr. 39/42 armor-piercing projectile. This projectile had a small explosive filler that detonated after penetrating the tank armor, significantly enhancing its chances of igniting an ammunition fire. It could penetrate about 168mm of RHA at 500m, more than adequate against the Sherman. During 1943, German industry produced about 18,800 rounds of the more potent Pzgr. 40/42 with a subcaliber tungsten carbide core, but production ended due to tungsten shortages, and it was seldom if ever used

The Sherman had a reputation for vulnerability to fires, wrongly attributed to its gasoline propulsion. German tanks, including the Panther, were gasoline powered, and the real culprit was ammunition propellant as seen in this fire on an M4A1 (76mm) of the 3rd Armored Division in Germany on March 1, 1945. (NARA)

in the Battle of the Bulge. Based on operational research during the war, the normal firing range for the Panther in combat was about 850m, while engagements at 1,400 to 1,750m occurred only about 5 percent of the time, and at ranges beyond that, hardly at all. The Panther's secondary armament consisted of three 7.62mm machine guns: in a ball mount in the hull, in a coaxial mount alongside the gun, and as an optional mount for air defense on the commander's cupola. The Wehrmacht did not place as much emphasis on machine guns as an offensive weapon as did the US Army, hence the lack of a heavy machine gun.

The standard antitank ammunition of the Sherman's 76mm M1A1 gun was the M62A1 armor-piercing projectile that could penetrate about 116mm of RHA at

The advent of the 76mm was an improvement in antitank firepower for the Sherman, as can be seen in this comparison of the rounds of the 75mm and 76mm gun in front of this new M4A3E8 of the 2nd Armored Division. (NARA)

500m. Like the German ammunition, it had a small 0.44-lb explosive charge to enhance its behind-armor effects. This projectile could not penetrate the Panther's glacis armor at any range and could only penetrate the turret mantlet reliably at ranges of 250yd or less. The 76mm gun could penetrate the Panther's side armor from more than 2,000yd; for the Sherman, typical combat ranges in the ETO were 890yd. The unexpectedly poor performance of the 76mm gun against the Panther in summer 1944 led to a crash program to improve the Sherman's ammunition. Gun chamber design limited short-term fixes because of the propellant volume, but the use of a subcaliber tungsten carbide penetrator in the new T4 high-velocity armor-piercing (HVAP) projectile and better propellant greatly increased speed and penetrating power, offering about 208mm of penetration at 500m compared to only 116mm on the M62 round. The first rounds were rushed to France in August 1944, but they were always in short supply due to the limited availability of tungsten carbide. US industry produced about 10,000 HVAP projectiles monthly until the end of the war, but M4A3 (76mm) tanks during the Battle of the Bulge seldom had more than one or two HVAP rounds on hand at any time. On paper, the Panther carried more ammunition than the Sherman: 82 rounds versus 71, but in practice the Sherman typically carried over 100 rounds in various nooks and crannies of the hull, while the Wehrmacht tended to be short on ammunition supplies.

The Sherman had better secondary armament than the Panther. Like the Panther, it had a .30cal machine gun in the hull for self-protection and coaxial to the main gun. However, the more powerful Browning M2 .50cal heavy machine gun was fitted on a turret pintle mount. While this weapon played no role in tank-versus-tank fighting, it was widely used against nearly every other type of target, especially enemy infantry and trucks. It was lauded by some US tank commanders such as Gen Bruce Clarke as the Sherman's "most important" weapon since it was used far more often than the main gun and was the best weapon of its type regularly used in tank combat in World War II. "I told my men that the greatest thing on the tank was a free .50cal. in the hands of the tank commander. We were not able to fight from tanks with the tank commander buttoned up – that has never been successfully done. [Buttoned up] he can't hear or see, and so pretty soon he unbuttons. Now if he's got a free .50cal machine gun, all he has to do is press his thumb and he can pick out a dangerous spot. It may be a bazooka flash or something. He can throw a burst there without even thinking about giving an order."

In terms of gun fire controls, both Sherman and Panther tanks had similar capabilities, with small advantages and disadvantages under different

The Sherman was prone to fire because it was vulnerable to penetration by nearly any of the Wehrmacht's antiarmor weapons from the infantry's panzerfaust through the 75mm and 88mm tank and antitank guns. Here the captain points to a penetration in the side hull of an M4A1 (76mm) of the 32nd Armored Regiment, 3rd Armored Division, which led to a catastrophic fire that burned the rubber off the tracks and wheels. This is an old Normandy veteran, with bits of the Douglas bocage cutter still evident on the bottom of the differential cover. (NARA)

PANTHER TURRET

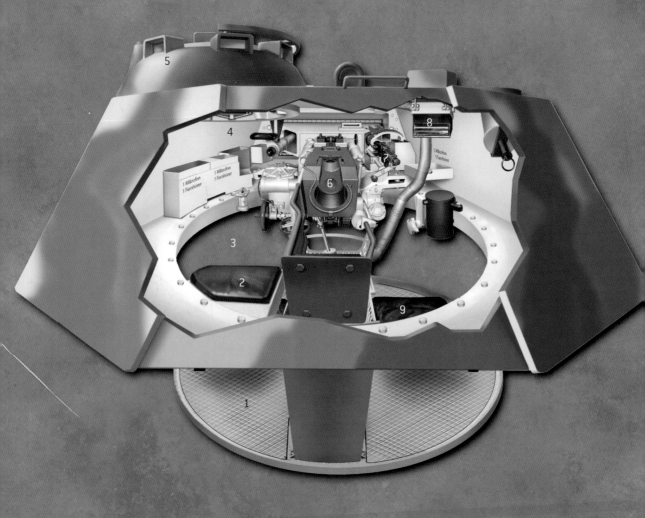

1. Sprenggranaten 42 (HE)
2. Panzergranate 39/42 (AP)

1. Rotating turret basket floor
2. Gunner's seat
3. Gunner's fire controls
4. Gunner's periscopic sight
5. Commander's vision cupola
6. 75mm gun
7. Co-axial machine gun
8. Loader's periscopic sight
9. Loader's seat

SHERMAN TURRET

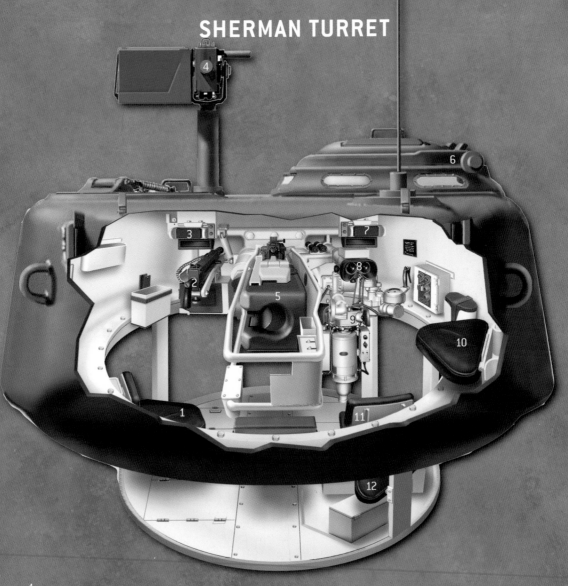

1. M42A1
2. Armor Piercing Capped (APC), M62A1
3. High Velocity Armor Piercing (HVAP)

1. Loader's seat
2. Co-axial .30cal machine gun
3. Loader's periscope
4. .50cal heavy machine gun
5. 76mm gun
6. Commander's all-vision cupola
7. Gunner's periscopic sight
8. Gunner's telescopic sight
9. Gunner's fire controls; turret traverse mechanism
10. Commander's folding travel seat
11. Gunner's seat
12. Commander's inside turret seat

circumstances. The Panther gunner was provided with a TFZ 12 telescope with 2.5x and 5x power magnification; this had better optical quality than the Sherman's 5x power M71D telescopic sight. The Sherman's main advantage was that the gunner was also provided with an M4 periscopic sight with an enclosed M47 telescope, which had a wide field of view that could be used for general observation prior to engaging a target. The Panther gunner lacked any secondary sighting device and had to rely on the lower 2.5x magnification view from the telescope, which had a very narrow field of view. As a result, it took about 20 to 30 seconds for a Panther gunner to engage after instructed by the commander, while the Sherman engagement cycle was considerably quicker. This gave an advantage to the Sherman in fast-moving, close-range engagements but was of little relevance in other circumstances; for example, if the Panther was waiting in ambush. One of the Sherman's more controversial features was the use of a one-axis gyrostabilizer. This was not precise enough to permit the Sherman to fire on the move but rather helped the gunner keep the reticle on-target during movement, so that when the tank stopped to fire, the gun would already be roughly aimed in the right direction. Gunners who had been extensively trained on maintaining the gyrostabilizer felt that it was a worthwhile feature, but due to combat attrition, more and more replacement gunners were not familiar with the system, and it fell into disuse in some units in late 1944.

The Sherman had other short-range advantages, including faster turret traverse. Both tanks used a power-assisted turret traverse, but the Panther traverse used a complicated power takeoff from the engine that depended on engine speed for maximum turret traverse speed while the Sherman's system was independent and faster. The Sherman turret traversed at about 25 degrees per second or a full 360-degree traverse in 15 seconds, while the Panther turret traversed at a maximum of about 15 degrees per second but only if the engine was at full power and the tank was on level ground. The Panther's slow turret traverse was aggravated by poor turret balance due to the long and heavy main gun tube and the absence of a turret bustle as fitted to American and Soviet tanks as a counterbalance. American turret crews considered the Sherman's fast turret traverse to be one of the few advantages they enjoyed, but this feature was useful only in close-range engagements.

Tank Gun Antiarmor Performance

Projectile type	500m*	1,000m*	Ammunition weight (lb)	Projectile weight (lb)	Propellant weight (lb)	Chamber pressure (psi)	Initial muzzle velocity (ft/sec)
76mm M62 APC**	116	106	24.8	15.4	3.62	38,000	2,600
76mm T4 HVAP	208	175	18.9	9.4	3.62	43,000	3,400
75mm Pzgr. 39/43 APCBC	168	149	31.5	15.0	8.17	46,400	3,065
17-pdr. APCBC	163	150	37.5	17.0	9.0	47,000	2,900
17-pdr. APDS	256	233	28.4	7.9	9.0	47,000	3,950

* Penetration in mm against armor at 0 degrees
** APC= armor-piercing capped, HVAP= high-velocity armor piercing, APCBC= armor-piercing capped with ballistic cap, APDS= armor-piercing discarding sabot

MOBILITY

The Panther was powered by a Maybach HL 230 P30 12-cylinder gasoline engine offering 600hp for a 15.5hp/ton power ratio. The M4A3 (76mm) was powered by a Ford GAA 8-cylinder gasoline engine offering 450hp for a 12.3hp/ton power ratio. The Panther had a slightly better power-to-weight ratio on paper, although in practice the difference was smaller due to the US use of good quality 80-octane gasoline, while the Wehrmacht was obliged to use inferior fuel, which degraded engine performance. The Panther had wide steel track offering a ground pressure of 12.3psi. The basic track used on the Sherman provided it with a 15.1psi ground pressure, which was poor for operations in muddy conditions. This led to the addition of "duckbill" extended end connectors to the track that lowered ground pressure to about 12.4psi, similar to the Panther. Most Shermans were fitted with duckbills by the time of the Battle of the Bulge. Introduction of the new M4A3E8 with 23-in. wide track lowered the ground pressure to 10.7psi, better than the Panther's. The Panther carried 190gal of gasoline, giving it an effective road range of about 60–80 miles and cross-country range of about 40–50 miles. Its fuel consumption was so high and Wehrmacht supplies so low that in summer 1944, Gen Heinz Guderian, the Inspector of the Panzer Force, sent a directive reminding commanders that "the large fuel consumption of Panthers makes it necessary to consider whether the mission is worth the cost." The M4A3 (76mm) carried 168gal of gasoline, giving it better endurance – a road range of about 100 miles and a cross-country range of about 65 miles.

The Panther continued to be plagued by mechanical durability problems due to transmission flaws and low durability. This Panther Ausf. G from III./Pz.Rgt.2, 2nd Panzer Division was abandoned near Clervaux, Luxembourg, in January 1945 due to engine problems. Most 2nd Panzer Division Panthers in the Ardennes were manufactured in November, and this example has the late-style, self-cleaning idler wheels, late flame dampers on the exhaust, and the crew compartment heater. (NARA)

A M4A3 (76mm) of the 750th Tank Battalion moves into Salmchateau in support of the 75th Division on January 16, 1945. The track is fitted with "duckbill," extended end connectors to improve flotation in mud.

Although the performance statistics between the Panther and Sherman do not reveal any startling differences, the Panther suffered from substantially poorer performance in the field due to weaknesses of the power train. The Panther's AK 7-200 transmission was an elegant design offering multigeared steering that permitted the Panther to pivot turn by running the tracks on one side in one direction and the other in the opposite direction, making it possible to spin the tank in place. While superficially attractive, the transmission was badly overstressed and suffered from premature stripping of the third gear. A more serious problem was the final drive, which had a nominal life expectancy of 1,500km, but which in practice was sometimes as low as 150km. The design was not adequate for a tank of this weight, and its single-teeth spur gears tended to strip more readily than the more robust double herringbone design used in the Sherman. To make matters worse, the pivot turn feature accelerated final drive failure in the hands of an inexperienced driver. These problems grew worse by the time of the Battle of the Bulge due to the growing alloy shortage that led to more brittle gears, declining quality control at factories, and the decline in spare parts production. While this situation was bad enough, the Panther transmission was fully enclosed by the front armor, meaning that to replace the final drive, the entire driver's compartment and transmission had to be disassembled to gain access to the faulty assembly.

The combination of premature transmission failure, time-consuming repair, and shortage of spare parts meant that Panther units in December 1944 were often understrength due to the significant number of sidelined tanks. On average, Panther units in 1944 had 35 to 40 percent of their tanks unavailable. At the outset of the Ardennes campaign, 29 percent of the Panthers were not operational, even though nearly all were new vehicles manufactured in September–November 1944. The Panther had a mechanical life expectancy of 1,500km (935 miles), although in practice this was rarely achieved either due to combat loss or mechanical problems. Panthers that suffered mechanical breakdowns in the field often were too difficult to repair in field conditions and so had to be abandoned. Of 47 Panther tanks in the Ardennes inspected by Allied intelligence after the fighting, 20 (42 percent) had been abandoned or destroyed by their crew. Although detailed statistics are lacking, a number of German prisoners of war indicated that Panther tank losses had been higher due to mechanical breakdown rather than enemy action. The durability of the Panther was so poor that long road marches were discouraged, and Panther units were generally moved by train if any significant distances were involved.

Mud was a bane to both US and German forces in autumn 1944 due to exceptionally heavy rainfall. This M4A3 of the 6th Armored Division fell victim to the mud and mines on November 25, 1944. The adoption of "duckbill" extended end connectors to the tracks improved, but did not eliminate, the problem, giving the M4A3 flotation comparable to the Panther. (NARA)

The ultimate solution for the Sherman's flotation problems was the new horizontal volute spring suspension (HVSS) with wider 23in. tracks. The first batch arrived in the Ardennes and was issued to the badly depleted 4th Armored Division, seen here near Bastogne on January 8, 1945. (NARA)

In contrast to the Panther, the M4A3 used a robust syncromesh transmission with controlled differential steering. In the event of transmission problems, access to the transmission was straightforward since the transmission was behind a cast-armored cover that could be unbolted and removed quickly. On the eve of the Battle of the Bulge, the US First Army had 10.6 percent of their Sherman tanks sidelined with mechanical problems, with the newer 76mm Shermans having better serviceability with only 5.9 percent sidelined. Even at the height of the Battle of the Bulge on Christmas Day 1944, the US First Army had less than 20 percent of its Sherman tanks sidelined with mechanical problems and battle damage.

The Sherman had a much longer mechanical life expectancy than the Panther. A survey conducted of Shermans by the US 3rd Armored Group in October 1944 found that those that had reached their 1,000-mile check were still in excellent mechanical condition; by this age, most Panthers would have exceeded their life expectancy. As a result, Shermans were regularly road marched long distances without excessive loss. US data on Sherman losses due to mechanical breakdown are rare, largely because the US Army recovered most broken-down tanks, and so their loss was only temporary. The durability of the Sherman greatly enhanced their combat value. The best example was the counterattack staged in the third week of December 1944 by the US Third and Ninth Armies, where several armored divisions conducted forced road marches of over 100 miles to reinforce the beleaguered US First Army. The 4th Armored Division, with no rest or refit after a month of fighting, was sent 130 miles in four days, the last 16 miles into Bastogne in intense combat.

THE COMBATANTS

PANTHER CREW

Both the Panther and Sherman had five crewmen with similar functions. The Panther tank commander (*Panzerführer*) was a lieutenant (*Leutnant*) if the platoon commander or an NCO (*Feldwebel, Unteroffizier*) in the remainder of the platoon. The Panther commander was stationed in the left rear of the turret below an armored cupola, with all-around vision via a set of seven periscopic sights. A seat was provided for while riding inside the turret; when riding outside the cupola, the commander stood on a small footrest, hinged on the empty-round bin. German tank commanders were regularly provided with a set of binoculars for long-range target search. The cupola had a simple frame mount for attaching an MG 34 light machine gun for antiaircraft defense, but the German tactics did not place as much emphasis on machine guns for use against ground targets as did the US Army. The Panther commander instructed his crew via an intercom system (*Fusprech*). In contrast to US and British practice, the radio was positioned in the hull next to the bow gunner, who operated the transceiver at the instructions of the commander.

Sitting in front of the commander was the gunner (*Richtschutze*), who was usually an NCO or senior enlisted man (*Unteroffizier, Obergefreiter*). The gunner sat in a cramped, claustrophobic position with the main gun against his right shoulder. A British motion study of the Panther concluded that "little consideration has been given in the design of these vehicles for the comfort of the gunner, and most of the crew's controls are so positioned as to be operated only with discomfort and fatigue." The gunner's main instrument was a TFZ 12a monocular telescopic sight. This did not have a brow pad, so it was not especially safe for the gunner to keep his eye to the sight during travel, and his head was so close to the gun assembly that he had to move his right earphone out of the way when sighting. The gunner did not have a periscopic sight for general observation during travel as did the Sherman. As a result, he depended on the commander for targeting instructions. This was not a significant problem when the Panther was static and looking for targets, but it slowed the firing cycle to about 20–30 seconds when the Panther had to engage targets from the move. On receiving the commander's instructions, the gunner first searched for the target using the 2.5x power magnification, then switching to 5x magnification for the engagement. The gunner flipped the reticle to the proper ammunition type depending on the commander's instructions and used the commander's range estimate to make the necessary elevation adjustment. In the case of Panthers with experienced gunners, the commander would usually leave the range estimate to the gunner. The gunner had two foot-operated controls for the hydraulic turret traverse and a backup wheel operated by his right hand in the event that the tank's engine was shut off. Gun elevation was by means of a wheel at the gunner's left hand. The gun trigger was located on the elevating wheel and discharged the gun electrically. When the gun fired, it ejected the spent casing back against a deflector plate that dropped it into a bin below. The bin automatically opened and shut to prevent fumes from filling the turret; a hose sucked fumes out of the turret. A British study concluded that "the gun arrangement in this vehicle is bad; the gun controls are badly positioned relative to the gunner's seat, the power traverse and elevating control are unsatisfactory to use."

The loader (*Ladeschutze*) stood in the right side of the turret during combat operations or sat on a small foldout seat attached to the empty-round bin. The position was relatively spacious compared to the left side of the turret, but as the space between the turret floor and roof was only 5' 3" high, most loaders had to crouch when servicing the main gun. The loader had a small episcope that covered the forward right quadrant of the tank, but he had no roof hatch, only a rear turret escape

Panther crew

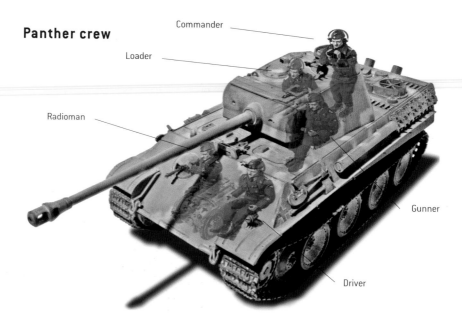

Commander

Loader

Radioman

Gunner

Driver

hatch. The ammunition stowage was adequate; when the gun was aimed straight ahead, the loader had access to two sponson racks and a rear rack for a total of 27 rounds. All other rounds were inaccessible to the gunner and would have to be passed to him by other crewmen or the turret traversed to provide access.

The driver (*Fahrer*) sat in the left front of the hull. Beginning in October 1944, the driver had a second seat added; the basic one was for operating the Panther in combat conditions with the hatch closed, and the new one was in an elevated location for road travel with the hatch open, the driver riding with his shoulders outside the hatch for better visibility. The driving controls could either be adapted for the closed and travel positions and consisted of steering levers on either side of the driver's legs, a gear lever, and a handbrake. After the commander and gunner, the driver was the most important and senior member of the crew since German practice was to encourage driver initiative in moving and positioning the tank, based on the commander's general instructions. When in closed combat position, the driver had a traversable periscope. This had been adopted on the Ausf. G in place of an opening armored hatch in front of the driver, which compromised the armor integrity of the glacis plate. British evaluations of this sight considered it inadequate.

The final member of the crew was the radio operator (*Funker*) who sat in the right front corner of the hull opposite the driver. His main role was to operate the tank's Fu 5 SE 10U radio transceiver, which was located to his left. The Fu 5 was an AM radio with two receivers, one with preset frequencies and the other to dial up channels. In addition to operating the radio, he also manned the bow machine gun, an MG 34 in a ball mount sighted through a KZF 2 cranked sight. Besides the machine gun sight, he also had an episcope which covered the right front quadrant of the tank. The position was not well configured as the episcope orientation prevented the gunner from using it to locate targets for the machine gun, and the machine gun sight had a very narrow field of view.

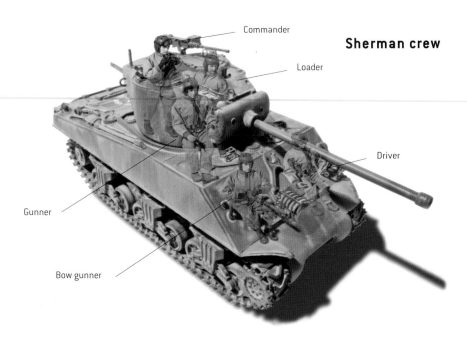

Commander

Loader

Sherman crew

Driver

Gunner

Bow gunner

SHERMAN CREW

In a Sherman platoon, the platoon leader was usually a 2nd lieutenant, the platoon sergeant was a staff sergeant, and the remaining commanders "buck" sergeants. The tank commander's station was on the right side of the turret and he had two seats, one at turret race level for riding inside the tank and the other a folding seat on the turret wall for riding outside the cupola. The cupola had six laminated glass vision ports for all-around vision, and the hatch had a fitting for either the standard M6 periscope or a 7x periscopic binocular. As in the Panther, the Sherman commander communicated with his men via the tank intercom. In contrast to the Panther, the commander in the M4A3 (76mm) had a remote control for the power turret traverse that allowed him to swing the turret in the direction of the target, if necessary. Another difference was that the US Army preferred to have the radio behind the commander in the bustle for his operation. In a standard tank platoon, the platoon leader and the platoon sergeant had the SCR-528, which included a transmitter and a receiver. The other three tanks had the SCR-538, which was only a receiver. In combat, the transmitters were usually salvaged from damaged or destroyed tanks, and many platoon leaders ended up with the SCR-508 combination, which basically was the SCR-528 but with a second transmitter added to permit the radios to be tuned simultaneously to the platoon net and the company or battalion net. The remaining SCR-538 were gradually upgraded through late 1944 to SCR-528 standards by adding a transmitter. In well-trained units, loaders were usually trained to assist the commander in operating the radio. The Sherman used FM radios, which were less susceptible to interference than the AM radios used on the Panther, particularly when used on the move. Many Shermans had also been retrofitted with field telephones on the rear wired into their intercom system, which enabled accompanying infantry to communicate directly with the crew and coordinate tactics; Panthers lacked this feature.

An M4 (76mm) of the 3rd Armored Division passes by an abandoned Panther Ausf. G of the 2nd SS-Panzer Division lost during the fighting near Grandmenil in the days around Christmas 1944. (NARA)

The gunner sat immediately in front of the commander in the M4A3 turret on the right-hand side. The gun controls were arranged differently than in the Panther. The gunner operated the gun elevation manually via a wheel with his left hand. Power traverse was by a joystick at his right hand and firing could be done either by a trigger on the joystick or by a button on the floor next to his feet. Like the Panther, the 76mm gun was semiautomatic and the spent casing was ejected on firing. Unlike the Panther, there was no elaborate stowage bin for the casing, and it simply fell into an open basket, and the turret fumes were extracted by means of a pair of ventilator fans. The gunner's sights in the Sherman were better than those in the Panther, consisting of an M4A1 periscope in the roof with a built-in M47A2 telescope, plus an M71D telescopic sight. The unitary periscope was an advantage since it allowed the gunner to maintain situational awareness while the tank was traveling by observing the terrain and looking for targets; the Panther gunner was essentially blind until the tank halted. The periscopic sight contained an aiming telescope, but against precision targets such as an enemy tank, the Sherman gunner would switch to the M71D telescope. This had only a 5x magnification and included illumination for the reticles for low-light conditions.

The loader was positioned in the left side of the turret and had a small folding seat when traveling that snapped up when loading the gun. The turret basket in the M4A3 (76mm) has small hatches on the floor under the loader's feet to allow him access to the ammunition racks below. The loader had 35 rounds of ammunition in angled tubes in the wet stowage bin below his feet as well as six more in a ready rack on the basket floor, giving him more readily accessible ammunition than his Panther counterpart. The remaining 30 rounds were stowed in a bin behind the bow gunner and had to be manually transferred when needed. Most US tank crews carried additional ammunition, typically in the sponsons. On the initial versions of the M4A3 (76mm), the loader's hatch was fitted with a mount for the tank's .50cal heavy machine gun, a change from previous Shermans, where this weapon was mounted on the commander's cupola. On the later production vehicles, the loader's hatch was changed from a large split hatch to a small oval hatch, and the machine gun was moved to an inconvenient pintle behind and between the loader's and commander's hatches, where it was difficult to use against ground targets. In many units, an additional pintle was welded in front of the commander and a .30cal machine gun was added for his use.

The driver sat in the left front corner of the hull. In combat with the hatch closed, vision was provided by a traversable periscope mounted in the hatch above plus a second fixed periscope in the hull roof. The Sherman used clutch-and-brake steering via control levers that was more akin to that of a tractor than an automobile. Besides actually driving the tank, the driver had to have a reasonably good appreciation of tactics and terrain, since in the heat of battle, the commander often depended on the driver's common sense to get the tank into the proper location, while minimizing its vulnerability to hostile fire.

The assistant driver was located in the right front of the hull next to the driver. He was primarily responsible for operating the .30cal hull machine gun, and so he was

GERMAN TANK ACES

The concept of "tank aces" was not particularly prevalent in World War II, even in the Wehrmacht. It was most common in the Waffen-SS, which was far more attuned to the propaganda imperatives of the Nazi state. It was especially common regarding the Tiger battalions, which enjoyed an envelope of invulnerability for one year, from summer 1943 to summer 1944, until the Allies finally fielded tanks, such as the T-34-85 and Sherman Firefly, that could defeat them. In Heer panzer units, the concept was not widespread, and military awards focused on mission performance, not an arbitrary metric like tank kills. Panther aces were far less common in German propaganda than Tiger aces as the Panther was far more vulnerable and had a much more troubled existence in its first year of service than did the Tiger. Tank kill claims during World War II on all sides should be taken with a grain of salt; the German Eastern Front intelligence service, Fremde Heere Ost, regularly cut claims in half to more accurately assess enemy losses. This was due not so much to account for deliberate inflation as it was to limit double counting when multiple tanks engaged a single enemy tank without knowledge of the others' actions or when a knocked out tank was "knocked out" again and again as other units moved through an area. The best known of the Panther aces of the Battle of the Bulge was Ernst Barkmann, who was a platoon leader in 4./SS-Pz.Rgt. 2 in the Ardennes. Barkmann joined the SS in 1936 and took part in the Polish and French campaigns in the infantry. He was seriously wounded during the Russian campaign in summer 1941. After serving as an instructor while convalescing, he joined the new Waffen-SS panzer force in early 1943, serving as a gunner on the PzKpfw III tank of Alfred Hargesheimer, who will figure in the duel later in this account. Following the battle of Kursk, Barkmann became a tank commander on one of the new Panther Ausf. D tanks and earned both classes of the Iron Cross during the fighting in Russia in late 1943. Barkmann was commander of a Panther Ausf. A tank when the 2nd SS-Panzer Division was deployed to Normandy, He came to prominence on July 27, 1944, when he

ambushed an American column near Le Lorey, claiming nine US Shermans and other vehicles, for which he was awarded the Knight's Cross.

During the Ardennes campaign, Barkmann took part in one of the most famous tank encounters of the battle, a wild nighttime melee against elements the 7th Armored Division retreating into Manhay on Christmas Eve. In his Panther Ausf G, Barkmann wandered into unsuspecting American columns, blasting a number of vehicles of the 40th Tank Battalion and the 48th Armored Infantry Battalion. Barkmann was wounded on Christmas but returned to the 2nd SS-Panzer Division in early 1945, taking part in the final campaigns in Hungary against the Red Army. By war's end, Barkmann claimed over 80 tanks to his credit.

At the center of the skirmish at Freyneux detailed below was another Panther commander of SS-Panzer Regiment 2, Fritz Langanke. Volunteering at 18, Langanke first served in the Germania Regiment as an infantryman in 1937 and transferred as a radio operator in an armored car in 1938. He was awarded the Iron Cross 2nd Class in December 1940 and the 1st Class in December 1941. His first combat in tanks took place in 1942, serving as a tank commander on the Eastern Front in a reconnaissance battalion until late 1943. Langanke was credited with one Russian tank kill. During a divisional reorganization, he became an ordnance officer in the I./SS-Pz.Rgt. 2 until D-Day, and during the fighting in Normandy, he served as a Panther commander and subsequently platoon commander with 2./SS-Pz.Rgt. 2, credited with 18 Allied tank kills during the Normandy fighting. He earned the Knight's Cross for his role in leading a breakout from the Roncey pocket of several dozen troops and a few tanks on the night of July 28, 1944.

The considerable attention paid to German tank aces in recent years obscures the fact that they were an exception to the rule and that most of the anonymous young German tankers in late 1944 were thrown into combat with poor training.

commonly called the "BOG" (bow gunner). He had the same type of vision periscopes as the driver, and since the machine gun lacked a dedicated sight, he aimed it by using tracer fire. The BOG's secondary function was to assist the loader by passing him ammunition from the hull stowage bin if needed. In the event that a crew was short one crewman, the BOG position was generally left unmanned as the least necessary crew position.

PANTHER CREW TRAINING

Both the Wehrmacht and US Army were beginning to run thin on tank crew replacements in winter 1944; the Wehrmacht being in poorer shape due to the horrible losses of the past summer on both fronts. While there were formal panzer crew training centers for both the Heer and Waffen-SS, the extreme shortages of personnel in autumn 1944

Ernst Barkmann was a platoon leader in IV./SS-Pz.Rgt. 2 during the Ardennes campaign and one of the top Panther aces of the war.

meant that most replacements were given minimal basic training and then sent to their panzer units for specialist training. There were three main sources of panzer crew trainees in autumn 1944: wounded veterans returning to service, new draftees, and displaced Luftwaffe and Kriegsmarine personnel. The latter category represented the best potential since in most cases the men were already accustomed to service life and had some form of military technical training.

The Wehrmacht had a fundamentally different replacement policy than the US Army in 1944. Divisions were kept in the line, receiving few replacements, with the combat elements shrinking into smaller and smaller *kampfgruppen* (battle groups). At some convenient point or when the division was decimated to point of uselessness, the entire unit would be pulled back for complete refitting. In the case of most of the panzer divisions deployed in the Ardennes, they were scoured out by the Normandy campaign and pulled out of the line in September 1944 for refitting. It should be kept in mind that in a typical wartime panzer division, about only one-third of the troops were engaged in direct combat, including the panzer crews, panzergrenadiers, and some other units such as the reconnaissance battalion. Of the 14,700 men in a Type 44 panzer division, about 2,000 were in the panzer regiment, of which about 750 were crewmen. Another 5,400 were in the two panzer grenadier regiments and reconnaissance battalion. Other elements such as the divisional engineers and artillery might occasionally be exposed to combat, but casualties tended to be heaviest in a narrow slice of the division. The administrative and support elements of the division tended to remain intact even in disasters such as the Falaise gap encirclement, and so divisions were rebuilt around an experienced core. When it is said that a division "suffered 50 percent casualties," these casualties were not evenly shared in the division and losses fell hardest on the combat elements. The panzer grenadier regiments tended to suffer worst of all due to the usual hazards of infantry combat combined with the mobility of these units, which led to their frequent commitment. Most of the panzer regiments lost one-third or more of their crewmen in Normandy and most if not all of their tanks.

The problem facing the Wehrmacht in the months before the Battle of the Bulge was that there was neither the time nor the resources to properly rebuild the divisions, and many corners were cut. In total, eight panzer divisions were assigned to the *Wacht am Rhein* operation, each equipped with a single panzer regiment and two panzergrenadier regiments. Although the Panther was supposed to completely replace the PzKpfw IV by 1944, shortages of the Panther led to the continued use of the older PzKpfw IV. Therefore, each panzer regiment nominally had a battalion each of Panther and PzKpfw IV. Of the eight panzer divisions eventually assigned to the Ardennes offensive, five were kept off-line for three months to refit. Three Heer divisions, the Panzer Lehr and the 9th and 116th Panzer Divisions, remained in combat until days before the offensive and hastily replenished.

The 1.SS-Panzer Division "Liebstandarte" provides a good example of the difficulties faced in reequipping and training the panzer regiments prior to the Ardennes offensive. The division had not been committed to Normandy until July and therefore suffered lower casualties than other Waffen-SS units such as 12.SS-Panzer Division, which was in action since D-Day. Liebstandarte was scoured of most of its heavy equipment during the fighting, and its Panther battalion, I./SS-Pz.Rgt. 1, lost nearly all its tanks in Normandy and about one-third of its men. Of the regiment's officers, its commander, Jochen Peiper, was in a hospital due to combat exhaustion, its two battalion commanders were hospitalized and would not return to the regiment, four company commanders were wounded, and one company commander and at least four platoon commanders had been killed. The division was pulled off the line in early September with plans to make it operational by the end of October. The I./SS-Pz.Rgt. 1 received its full complement of new recruits, but the standards of late 1944 were not comparable to previous years and the Waffen-SS received draftees as well as volunteers. The new recruits had undergone basic training, but specialist training had been minimal, and few of the trainees had never been in a tank or fired a tank gun. Driver training was elementary, with only two hours of actual armored vehicle driving necessary to receive a license, usually on obsolete tanks. Under the new reduced tables of equipment, I./SS-Pz.Rgt. 1 initially had two companies of Panther tanks (17 each) plus command tanks for a total of 38 Panthers while its counterpart second battalion had PzKpfw IV tanks. Tank shortages meant that the four companies were merged into a mixed battalion instead of the usual pattern of one Panther and one PzKpfw IV battalion. Since the 1.SS-Panzer Division and its neighbor, the 12.SS-Panzer Division, were assigned the principal route of the attack, they were given a battalion of Tiger II heavy tanks instead of a standard full-strength panzer regiment.

The battalion did not receive its new Panthers until mid-October at Grafenwöhr. Training began at Wietzendorf in the final week of October 1944. The training was compromised by an almost total lack of fuel and ammunition. Gunnery training consisted of dry runs, with occasional use of coaxial machine guns. The surviving veterans of the Normandy fighting attempted to impart as much practical knowledge as possible to the new recruits. Only one actual live firing exercise was conducted, in early November. The regiment was transferred by train to its forward deployment area around Weilerwist from November 14–18, 1944. Training continued in this area but continued to be hampered by a lack of fuel, preventing any exercises above platoon level. Live fire was out of the question, and strict radio silence limited training in this area as well. Since the cover story for the deployment was to defend the area against an expected Allied advance, the training focused on defensive tactics. The Panther companies were finally moved forward by road on the night of December 13/14, 1944, to the area in the Blankenheim forest a short distance from the front line.

Fritz Langanke was a platoon commander in II./SS-Pz. Rgt. 2 during the Ardennes campaign and at the center of the Freyneux skirmish detailed here.

The 1.SS-Panzer Division's partner in the Ardennes attack was the 12.SS-Panzer Division "Hitlerjugend," which escaped from Normandy with heavy losses, including over 4,400 wounded and more than 4,000 killed or captured. It had lost nearly 75 percent of the troops in its two panzergrenadier regiments. Its Panther regiment, I./SS-Pz.Rgt. 12, had lost over 40 percent of its men and was moved to lower Saxony in October 1944 to refit. Replacements came from SS replacement units as well as Luftwaffe and Kriegsmarine troops freed up by the fuel shortages. Like SS-Pz.Rgt. 1, it received only enough replacement tanks in October–November 1944 to equip four tank companies instead of eight and so had to amalgamate them into a hybrid Panther/PzKpfw IV battalion. The Panther companies faced the same difficulties: little fuel or ammunition for training and no batteries for training radiomen. However, the divisional commander believed that SS-Pz.Rgt. 12 was in adequate shape, with "good and front-tested soldiers, NCOs, and officers." His main worry was the panzergrenadier regiment and reconnaissance battalion, which were not ready for combat when the division was moved westward in mid-November 1944.

The 2.SS-Panzer Division "Das Reich" had escaped from Normandy with relatively modest combat casualties of 4,000, though it had suffered especially heavy casualties in SS-Pz.Rgt. 2 of about 40 percent and most of its heavy equipment lost in the Roncey pocket. In contrast to the two previous SS-Panzer Regiments, it received no Panther tanks until late November. However, it was eventually refitted with four companies of Panthers, so that I./SS-Pz.Rgt. 2 went into combat in the Ardennes at full strength; its second battalion was full strength but with two of its four companies substituting StuG III assault guns for PzKpfw IV tanks. The belated arrival of its Panther tanks compromised the training of the new recruits, but the division was in significantly better shape than the two Waffen-SS panzer divisions of 1.SS-Panzer Korps. The officer casualties suffered in Normandy led to most command positions being filled by elevating combat leaders one step. The Panther battalion commander, Obersturmbannführer Rudolph Enseling, was elevated to command of the entire SS-Pz.Rgt. 2 due to the death of Christian Tyschen. Enseling was replaced by 26-year-old Wilhelm Matzke. Panther company commanders were new as well: Obersturmführer Karl Muhlek with I./SS-Pz.Rgt. 2 and Alfred Hargesheimer with 2./SS-Pz.Rgt. 2.

The 2.SS-Panzer Division's partner in the 2.SS-Panzer Korps was 9.SS-Panzer Division "Hohenstaufen," which had suffered heavier losses than any of the other Waffen-SS divisions among its panzer troops in Normandy, extricating barely one-third of its panzer crew. It was sent to the quiet Arnhem region in the Netherlands to rest and refit, only to become enmeshed in the famous battle for the "Bridge too Far" in September 1944. It did not receive its replacement Panther tanks until late November 1944 and so had little time for proper training of its new tank crews, which constituted more than half of its men.

Of the four Heer panzer divisions of the 5th Panzer Army, the 2.Panzer Division was among the best equipped for the Ardennes offensive. The division had emerged badly scarred from Normandy, losing more than half the troops in Pz.Rgt. 3 and most of its tanks. It was moved to the Fallingbostel area for refitting and began receiving new Panthers at the end of October. Panzer Lehr's Pz.Rgt. 130 had been crushed by the Allied bombing attacks at the beginning of Operation *Cobra* on July 24, 1944, but had been partially rebuilt after Normandy and brought back to full strength in November 1944, with the usual problems of too little fuel and ammunition for proper training of new recruits. Both the 9th and 116th Panzer Divisions remained in combat against the US Army in the fighting from September to early December 1944 along the Siegfried Line. They had generally been kept near

Sgt Lafayette Poole of the 32nd Armored Regiment, 3rd Armored Division was commander of the tank named "In the Mood," seen here during a bridge crossing operation on the Belgian frontier in September 1944, a few weeks before it was knocked in the fighting for Stolberg. (NARA)

full strength in November 1944 in anticipation of the Ardennes offensive, and they were given a short break in early December to refit and fill out their ranks. Although they were the most battle-hardened and experienced panzer divisions serving in the Ardennes, there is a thin line between battle hardened and battle weary. Besides these eight panzer divisions with Panther tanks, a few other German units in the offensive also had Panthers, including the panzer battalion of the Führer Grenadier Brigade and and Skorzeny's Panzer Brigade 150. Skorzeny's Panthers were the most curious because his unit had the task of impersonating US troops to gain control of key bridges by guile rather than combat. The unit's five Panther tanks were disguised as US Army M10 tank destroyers.

SHERMAN CREW TRAINING

In general, the US Army enjoyed better crew training than the Wehrmacht because many units were formed in 1942 and didn't go into combat until summer 1944, providing ample time for the crew to become familiar with their responsibilities. Indeed, most tank crews had so much time in training that they were often cross-trained on other positions, which proved useful when casualties occurred and positions needed to be filled quickly. The formal process was to send future tankers to the Armored Force Replacement Training Center (AFRTC) at Ft Knox, Kentucky, after basic training, although the limited number of slots there forced the Army to send many future tankers directly to their assigned units where they received their specialist training. The US Army stationed the 707th Tank Battalion in Britain with the Ground Force Replacement System in 1943, which provided additional specialist training prior to deployment to Europe. However, the demand for tank battalions was so great that this unit was sent to the First Army in September 1944 and would end up in the thick of the fighting in the Ardennes. The US replacement system was designed to keep units on the line indefinitely, and individual replacements were fed in as needed, with an aim to keeping the units at close to full strength.

Much of the American tactical training was not realistic because so few US tank units had seen combat until June 1944. This lack of realism led to high tank casualties in the first few weeks of combat; in separate tank battalions, the units often suffered half of their total wartime tank casualties within their first few weeks of combat. To improve this situation, the armored groups in the US 12th Army Group began setting up meetings in autumn 1944 between newly arrived tank battalions and experienced tank battalions to permit the combat veterans to pass on critical "lessons learned" to the green troops. For example, when the 707th Tank Battalion arrived in the ETO in October 1944, key personnel were sent to visit the veteran 70th Tank Battalion, which had been in action since the 1942 Tunisia campaign. By the time of the Ardennes campaign, nearly all of the US tank units had already become battle experienced, with a few exceptions, such as the 11th Armored Division, which was first committed to combat in January 1945 in the fighting around Bastogne.

The crew of an M4A3 (76mm) command tank of Capt John Megglesin of the 42nd Tank Battalion, 11th Armored Division cross their fingers for luck. This new tank was the third they had been issued in two weeks of fighting. The two previous tanks had been knocked out, fortunately without the loss of a single crewman. It was a grim statistic that on average, one crewman was killed every time a Sherman tank was knocked out.

US tank units suffered higher attrition in summer 1944 than had been expected, so there were often shortages of replacements with the proper skills. However, this was not on the scale of the casualties suffered by the Wehrmacht. Average casualties in the separate tank battalions in the ETO for the 11 months of combat from June 1944–May 1945 were 65 killed/missing in action and 185 wounded in action. The highest casualties suffered by any of the separate battalions was the 70th Tank Battalion with 166 killed/missing in action and 530 wounded in action, of an average strength of 750 men. This unit had been in combat in Tunisia and Sicily and had landed on D-Day, which accounts for its higher-than-average casualties. But to put this in perspective, the worst US tank unit casualties in more than two years of fighting were lower than average German panzer regiment casualties in less than three months of Normandy fighting.

UNIT ORGANIZATION

On paper, the Type 44 panzer division had a single panzer regiment with a battalion of 76 Panthers and a battalion of 76 PzKpfw IV tanks, plus three Panther and five PzKpfw IV command tanks in the regimental HQ company. As is evident from the tables presented here, none of the Panther regiments taking part in the Ardennes operation were at authorized strength due to continuing shortages of tanks. Each battalion had four tank companies, numbered 1 to 4 in the 1st (Panther) Battalion and 5 to 8 in the 2nd (PzKpfw IV) Battalion. Once again, tank shortages led to modified tables of organization. Each Panther battalion had four companies with 17 Panthers organized into four five-tank platoons. The Wehrmacht in 1944 could not afford to attach tank battalions to infantry divisions for support but instead used assault guns such as the StuG III or Jagdpanzer 38 (t).

The US Army had a significantly denser employment of tanks than the Wehrmacht, using them not only in armored divisions but also in separate tank battalions attached to infantry divisions for support. Typically, a US infantry division in combat would have an attached tank battalion and an attached tank destroyer battalion. US tank battalions under the November 1944 table of organization had three Sherman medium tank companies (A, B, C) and a M5A1 light tank company (D) with a total of 53 Sherman medium tanks and 17 M5A1 light tanks. There were an additional six M4 (105mm) assault guns, which were Sherman tanks mounting a 105mm howitzer for fire support. Three of these were in the HQ company and one each in the medium tank companies. As in the German case, each tank platoon consisted of five tanks. US armored divisions in the Ardennes were generally based on the 1943 tables of organization and equipment (TO&E) with three battalions each of tanks, armored infantry, and armored field artillery. The exceptions were the 2nd and 3rd Armored Divisions, which remained on a modified version of the old 1942 "heavy" TO&E with two tank regiments, each with three tank battalions for a total of six per division.

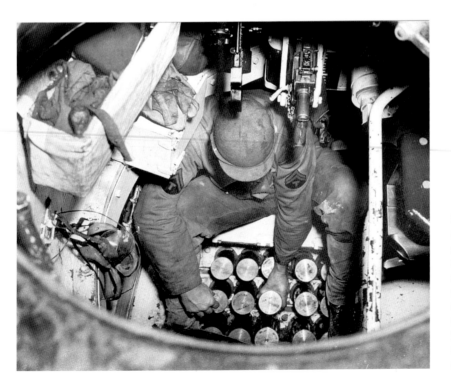

One of the most significant changes on the second-generation Shermans such as the M4A3 (76mm) was the use of wet ammunition stowage, which moved the ammunition from the vulnerable sponsons into a less vulnerable location in the hull floor and encased them in a thinly armored bin. (NARA)

US TANK ACES

Tank aces did not exist in the US Army in World War II. This does not mean that no tank crews had scored more than five enemy tank kills; rather the concept did not exist, and efforts to create such a category were routinely squashed by senior officers. The first likely candidate for tanker stardom was Sgt Lafayette Poole of Company I, 3/32nd Armored, 3rd Armored Division. Poole's tank, "In the Mood," was credited with destroying 258 German vehicles, of which one-third may have been armored vehicles of various types. He was seriously wounded during the fighting for Stolberg in mid-September 1944, losing a leg when his tank was knocked out. Poole was nominated at least twice for the Medal of Honor, but he was rejected both times by divisional officers since the honor singled out the tank commander for team effort of the tank crew. Poole was instead awarded the Distinguished Service Cross and the Silver Star for his personal actions.

Lt Col Creighton Abrams is sometimes regarded as the top US tank ace of the war, but his many military honors came for his exemplary leadership of the 37th Tank Battalion rather than for the number of panzers destroyed. (Patton Museum)

Probably the highest-scoring tank commander in the US Army was Col. Creighton Abrams, commander of the 37th Tank Battalion, 4th Armored Division. Abrams' tank, "Thunderbolt," had the reputation in his battalion as the high scorer, and this particular battalion saw an unusually large amount of tank-versus-tank fighting, including the largest single tank-versus-tank engagement of US Army in the ETO, at Arracourt in September 1944. Abrams attributed the high score of his tank to his excellent gunner, Sgt John Gatusky. His tank crew may have destroyed about 50 German AFVs, but no one ever bothered to keep count as it was not considered significant. By the end of the war, the 31-year-old Abrams had won two Distinguished Service Crosses, two Silver

Stars, a Bronze Star for valor, and the Legion of Merit. Gen George S. Patton later remarked, "I'm supposed to be the best tank commander in the Army, but I have one peer – Abe Abrams. He's the world's champion." Abrams won this accolade not because of the number of tanks his crew had knocked out but because of his exemplary tactical skill on the battlefield on a wide range of missions. Many US tankers were recognized for their battlefield performance with the Silver Star, Distinguished Service Cross, or other awards, but seldom if ever for the number of panzers they had knocked out.

THE STRATEGIC
SITUATION

By autumn 1944, Germany was in a desperate position after the catastrophic defeats of the summer on both the Eastern and Western Fronts. The German war industry was on borrowed time, having lost access to petroleum supplies in Romania and other critical materials. Hitler decided on a final gamble in the Ardennes, hoping to drive the allies out to the sea at Antwerp, trapping the British 21st Army Group and forcing another Dunkirk. The operation was first misleadingly codenamed *Wacht am Rhein* (Watch on the Rhine) to suggest it was a defense against an Allied Rhine crossing, and it was renamed *Herbstnebel* (Autumn Mist) in the days before its start. German commanders had little confidence in the plan due to the threadbare condition of the Wehrmacht in the west. The plan had one major factor in its favor – the feeble US defenses in the Ardennes. Bradley's 12th Army Group was so short of infantry divisions that it was obliged to leave some sectors thinly defended. The Ardennes was considered the least risky option as the hilly and forested terrain made it an unattractive target for a German attack. As a result, only four infantry divisions were stationed there in early December 1944: the 4th and 28th Divisions, which were recuperating after having been crippled during the savage Hürtgen Forest battles, and two green divisions, the 99th and 106th, which had just arrived in the area days before.

The German attack force consisted of three armies: Brandenburger's 7th Army in the south, Manteuffel's 5th Panzer Army in the center, and Dietrich's 6th (SS) Panzer Army in the north. Hitler placed the emphasis on the right wing with Sepp Dietrich's 6th Panzer Army since this area was closest to the main objective of Antwerp. Distrusting the senior Heer commanders since the July bomb plot, Hitler had more confidence in the Waffen-SS and so assigned two SS panzer corps to Dietrich's force

The shortage of Panthers led to substitutions. The low, sleek Jagdpanzer IV was first designed as an expedient tank hunter, combining the Panther's gun and thick armor in a fixed casemate on the PzKpfw IV hull. But in late 1944 and early 1945, some tank battalions began receiving "Guderian's Duck" as a tank substitute under its new designation PzKpfw IV/70 to make up for the continuing shortage of Panthers. As the slogan on the side attests, this one was lost in fighting with the 3rd Armored Division. (NARA)

including four Waffen-SS panzer divisions. While these did not have substantially more tanks than the neighboring Heer formations, they were reinforced with two of the scarce King Tiger heavy tank battalions. Manteuffel's neighboring 5th Panzer Army also had two panzer corps with four panzer divisions, but two of these, the 9th and 116th Panzer Divisions, had little time to refit after a hard autumn's campaigning along the Siegfried line further north. Brandenburger's 7th Army was an infantry force assigned to cover the flank of the two main assault forces and so had no panzer divisions.

For the attack to succeed, the lead units had to reach the Meuse (Maas) River in four days, X+3. The plan called for the infantry divisions to break through the thin US defenses on X-Day, December 16, 1944, at which point the panzer divisions would be unleashed to race for the Meuse. The Panther battalions in each of the eight panzer divisions had an especially prominent role to play, as they were assigned as the spearheads of the Ardennes attack. If they failed to quickly reach the Meuse River, the German commanders had few doubts that the US Army would shift massive reinforcements into Belgium and crush the attack.

The Waffen-SS had weak leadership at its senior levels, often chosen for loyalty over military competence. Capabilities in the Ardennes were further impaired by its lack of experience in offensive operations. The Waffen-SS had expanded during 1943–44 during a period when Germany was on the defensive. Although the Waffen-SS had a hard-won reputation for tenacious defense, the Heer commanders were skeptical of their offensive skills of the Waffen-SS. This was evident in the way they misused reconnaissance battalions and neglected engineers, key tools in offensive operations.

Tactical planning for the Ardennes operation was complicated by the contradictions between loyalty to Hitler's whims and military experience. Hitler insisted that the offensive begin with a crushing artillery barrage against the US

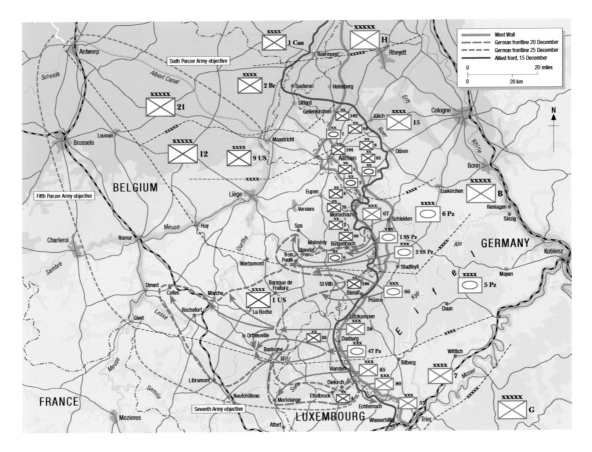

An operations map illustrating the German attack in the Ardennes, December 16–25, 1944.

positions. The Heer commanders were skeptical that enough artillery would be available, and from the fighting in the neighboring Hürtgen Forest, it was evident that artillery was not lethal enough against troops in wooden shelters like those the Americans had dug along the forward lines. The Heer generals, such as Manteuffel, preferred to follow the hard-learned lessons from 1917–18 and the Eastern Front to infiltrate the enemy positions without artillery rather than simply alert them with an ineffective barrage. This drama played itself out in the early morning hours of X-Day, with Dietrich's 6th Panzer Army following Hitler's misbegotten instructions and Manteuffel surreptitiously dodging them.

The popular perception of the Battle of the Bulge is a winter engagement across snow-covered hills. In reality, the first week of the campaign was fought in cold mud with temperatures hovering around freezing with rain mixing with snow showers. Autumn 1944 had seen twice as much rain as average, and the farm fields along the German border were a muddy morass. The attacking German forces soon learned that any tank venturing off the roads would quickly become trapped in the mire. As a result, panzer attacks had to be conducted down the roads, and so the many little villages dotting the Ardennes became the critical resistance points for the US defense of the Ardennes during the first week of fighting.

COMBAT

PANTHER GRAVEYARD: KRINKELT-ROCHERATH

The northernmost panzer division was the 12.SS-Panzer Division, waiting for the 277th Volksgrenadier Division (VGD) to break through two battalions of the green US 99th Division. When they failed to do so on X-Day, the 12.SS-Panzer Division used a kampfgruppe from SS-Panzergrenadier Regiment 25 supported by Jagdpanzer IV tank destroyers to stiffen the attack. After a costly day of fighting, the German force battled its way out of the woods and headed for the twin village of Krinkelt-Rocherath, only a few kilometers from the border. In the meantime, the US Army had sent the battered 1st Battalion, 9th Infantry of the 2nd Infantry Division to sacrifice themselves at the Lausdell crossroad on the approaches to the village to buy time for reinforcements to arrive. Elements of the German kampfgruppe managed to infiltrate into the village, but the growing tempo of US artillery from the neighboring Elsenborn ridge and the tenacious defense of the crossroads prevented a breakthrough. By X+2, the 12.SS-Panzer Division commander became impatient and sent in his two Panther companies in the hopes of finally cracking the defenses. It was against German doctrine to use Panthers in built-up areas, even more so without adequate panzergrenadier support, but the division was badly behind schedule and desperate for a breakthrough. The Panthers attacked in the predawn hours, losing four tanks at the crossroads to mines and artillery fire. Brushing past the crossroads, the Panthers fought their way into the villages, losing most of the supporting panzergrenadiers to artillery and small arms fire.

On December 18, the village was defended by the 38th Infantry Regiment supported by about 20 Sherman tanks of the 741st Tank Battalion, none of them armed with the 76mm gun, and a number of M10 tank destroyers. In the confined quarters of the village, the Panthers stumbled into ambush after ambush, losing six Panthers in the opening stage of the battle to Shermans hidden in alleyways and behind buildings. More fell victim to infantry with bazookas and 57mm antitank guns. The fight for Krinkelt-Rocherath continued through the evening with German reinforcements from the 12th VGD trying to pry the American infantry out of the village, with little success. By the afternoon of December 19, when the 38th Infantry finally withdrew, the two companies of the 741st Tank Battalion had claimed 27 panzers, two Jagdpanzer IV, two armored cars, and two half-tracks at a cost of eight tanks. M10 tank destroyers of the 644th Tank Destroyer (TD) Battalion claimed 16, regimental 57mm guns claimed 19, and bazooka teams claimed 37. The American defenders claimed over 100 destroyed German tanks in total, clearly an exaggeration, but an estimate that gives some idea of the ferocity of the fighting. While there are no precise figures from the German side, the Panther companies were crippled and played little role in subsequent fighting. When the 12.SS-Panzer Division continued its attempts to break through at the Dom Butgenbach manor farm on December 20, the tank support for the attack came primarily from the attached Jagdpanther battalion as well as surviving PzKpfw IV tanks and Jagdpanzer IV tank destroyers. This second attack was stopped after three days of fighting, on December 22, by the 26th Infantry Regiment supported by a Sherman company from the 745th Tank Battalion, ending the advance of the 12.SS-Panzer Division.

The other panzer spearhead of the 1.SS-Panzer Korps was 1.SS-Panzer Division, with the Panther companies part of the Kampfgruppe Peiper vanguard. As in the case of the 12.SS-Pz. Division, the penetration of the initial US infantry defenses along the frontier did not proceed on schedule, leading the frustrated 1.SS-Panzer Division to

This Panther belonged to the reconnaissance platoon of the SS-Pz.Rgt. 12 headquarters and was knocked out in the outskirts of Krinkelt-Rocherath during the fighting there on December 19. (Bill Auerbach)

A photo taken after the savage fighting inside Krinkelt shows a pair of Panthers of the 12.SS-Panzer Division destroyed near the village church. The Panther in the foreground, tactical number 318 of Hauptsturmführer Kurt Brödel, has lost its gun barrel. (NARA)

commit Kampfgruppe Peiper behind schedule. Kampfgruppe Peiper reached Stavelot on the late afternoon of X+1, December 17, shortly before the arrival of the first US reinforcements from the 30th Division. Kampfgruppe Peiper pushed through Stavelot to La Gleize the following day with the Panther companies in the vanguard, but Stavelot had not been cleared of US infantry, and the spearhead would soon be cut off from the bulk of the division. By this stage, Kampfgruppe Peiper's tank strength had been reduced to 23 Panthers, six PzKpfw IV, one Wirbelwind, and six Tiger II, mainly due to breakdowns and diversion of tanks on secondary missions. A company of Panther tanks managed to wrest control of Stoumont from the 30th Division on December 19, only to be pushed back out later in the day. This was the high watermark for 1.SS-Panzer Division, and Kampfgruppe Peiper remained trapped in La Gleize as US reinforcements closed in on the village. Kampfgruppe Peiper was forced to abandon its heavy equipment and withdraw on Christmas Eve.

The failure of the two vanguard Waffen-SS panzer divisions to secure a breakthrough doomed the German plans. The best routes to the Meuse River were blocked by determined US infantry backed by modest numbers of Sherman tanks. Both Panther battalions were decimated, the SS-Pz.Rgt. 1 was forced to abandon most of their Panthers around La Gleize, and SS-Pz.Rgt. 12 lost most of theirs in the savage street fighting in Krinkelt-Rocherath. As a result, the follow-up attack by 2.SS-Panzer Korps had to be shifted from this sector further south, where the Wehrmacht had enjoyed greater success breaking through the frontier. But the delay in committing the other two SS panzer divisions meant that they would face substantially greater US reinforcements, including a much more substantial tank force.

BREAKTHROUGH TOWARD BASTOGNE

While the 6th Panzer Army was stymied in its attempts to secure a breakthrough in the northern sector, Manteuffel's 5th Panzer Army succeeded due to a better use of its infantry. Against orders, Manteuffel scouted the area beforehand and recognized the vulnerability of the newly arrived 106th Division. Before the start of the mandatory artillery barrage, he infiltrated two infantry regiments around the forward defenses of the 106th Division. The eventual encirclement and capture of these two regiments led to a gaping hole in the American defenses. The other US division in this sector, the 28th Division, had been badly beaten up in the Hürtgen Forest fighting a month earlier and was still recuperating. Badly outnumbered, its regiments put up a stiff defense, backed up by the 707th Tank Battalion. Like the other separate tank battalions in the Ardennes sector, it was equipped with 75mm Shermans and no 76mm tanks. Over the course of four days, the 28th Division and the 707th Tank Battalion fought a series of harrowing battles, gradually falling back on the crossroad town of Bastogne. Two panzer divisions, the 116th Panzer Division toward Houfallize and the 2nd Panzer Division toward Bastogne, began to exploit the gaps in the frontier – in both cases with their Panthers following their divisional reconnaissance battalions.

The sacrifice of the 28th Division gave the US First Army time to move in reinforcements. The first to arrive were combat commands of two armored divisions sent to retrieve the surrounded 106th Division. Combat Command B (CCB) 9th Armored Division consisted of the usual mix of one tank, one armored infantry, and

The separate tank battalions supporting the US infantry divisions along the Belgian border were equipped mainly with the 75mm Sherman. The 707th Tank Battalion was attached to the embattled 28th Divison, and one of its M4A3 tanks can be seen knocked out behind a StuG III assault gun in the village of Clervaux after the fighting. (NARA)

An M4A3 (76mm) tank of the 7th Armored Division supports the 23rd Armored Infantry Battalion during the capture of the town of Hunnage on the way back to St Vith on January 23, 1945.

one armored field artillery battalion, and its 14th Tank Battalion was the first M4A3 (76mm) battalion to see extensive combat in the Ardennes. The 7th Armored Division began moving in from the Netherlands, and its CCB was deployed to St Vith. These formations plus remnants of the 28th and 106th Divisions held the St Vith salient through December 23 "like a thumb down the German throat." This was a major obstruction between the 5th and 6th Panzer Armies and prevented a coordinated German exploitation of the ruptures in the American line. Most of the fighting in this sector by the American tank battalions was against German infantry, in some cases reinforced by a few tanks or assault guns.

HARD GROUND, ANGRY SKIES

On December 23, the end of the first week of the offensive, the 5th Panzer Army had managed to penetrate the US lines and reach Bastogne, held by the newly arrived 101st Airborne Division, while 6th Panzer Army was still stymied in the northern sector. The weather had turned much colder with the arrival of a "Russian high," a cold weather front from the east, on the night of December 22/23. This had immediate tactical implications for the German attack. On one hand, it greatly benefited the attack since the ground froze hard and enabled the Panthers to get off the roads and move cross-country again. This gave the lead panzer elements much greater tactical mobility since they could now easily avoid the thinly stretched American defense that had coalesced in the towns and villages. On the other hand, it also meant that the skies turned from overcast to clear and were soon swarming with American fighter-bombers. The panzer divisions' vital supply elements were the sudden victims of "Thunderbolt hell." While Bastogne was a nettlesome thorn in the rear of the 5th Panzer Army, the other major road obstruction was cleared when CCB 9th Armored Division and CCB 7th Armored Division were given permission to withdraw from St Vith when it became obvious that their positions were untenable. Combined with the winter weather, this gave the 2nd SS-Panzer Korps the opportunity it was waiting for. Its 2nd and 9th SS-Panzer Divisions were redirected toward the center of the advance and sent racing toward the high ground of the Tailles Plateau and to the Meuse River beyond.

What was not obvious at the time was that 5th Panzer Army breakthrough was a race to nowhere. With the fastest routes to the Meuse blocked in the 6th Panzer Army sector, Manteuffel's Heer panzer divisions were headed along much more lengthy approach routes far from the Meuse. The time factor would prove absolutely critical as it gave the US opportunity to move its more mobile armored divisions into the Ardennes. To the south, George Patton's Third Army had been preparing a major drive in the Saar called Operation *Tink*. Ready for offensive action, one of his corps was aimed northward instead of eastward, aimed for Bastogne. To the north, Gen. "Lightning Joe" Collins' VII Corps was assigned the US Army's two most powerful armored divisions, the 2nd and 3rd Armored Divisions, each of which had six tank battalions instead of the usual three. The VII Corps would form the core of the second counterattack force, moving along the high ground of the Tailles Plateau. These two divisions would be at the center of the greatest tank battles of the Ardennes: the 3rd Armored Division intercepting the 2nd SS-Panzer Korps before it could make its way through the hill country beyond Manhay and the 2nd Armored Division crashing into the spearheads of 5th Panzer Army beyond Bastogne on Christmas.

The pullback of the 7th Armored Division from the St Vith salient coincided with the arrival of two combat commands of the 3rd Armored Division around the key

This Panther Ausf. G of the 116th Panzer Division was knocked out by the 3rd Armored Division during the fighting for Hotton on December 26 along with a PzKpfw IV, tactical number 611, in the background. The Panther is a new production tank built no earlier than October 1944, judging from the crew compartment heater cowling on the rear engine deck.

A pair of 3rd Armored Division Shermans in the Ardennes with a veteran M4A1 (76mm) on the left and one of the heavily armored M4A3E2 assault tanks on the right. (NARA)

crossroad of Manhay. Closely following behind was the 2nd SS-Panzer Division, which pushed to the fringes of Manhay on December 23. An attempt to take Manhay from the southwest by two companies of Panthers on the morning of Christmas Eve was frustrated as will be recounted in more detail below. On Christmas Eve, while the 7th Armored Division was attempting to reposition its defenses south of Manhay, the other two companies of Panthers of SS-Panzer Regiment 2 struck, shooting up several US

PANTHER GUNSIGHT VIEW

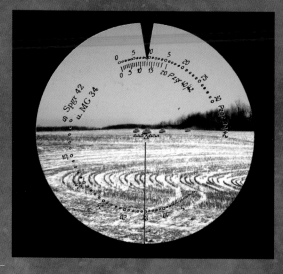

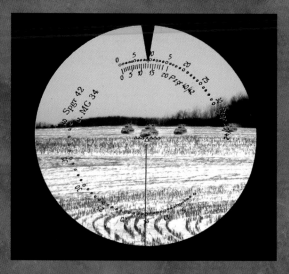

A view of Sherman tanks through a TFZ 12a set at 2.5 power. The enemy tank is 900m away.

The view through the same gunsight but set at 5 power shows a much clearer view of the enemy tanks.

columns in the moonlight and pushing into Manhay. For the next several days, 3rd Armored Division fought a series of violent battles with 2nd SS-Panzer Division around Manhay and Grandmenil and against 116th Panzer Division around Hotton and Soy. The road junctions in these towns were a critical bottleneck to the roads to Liège since the hills were forested and inaccessible by tanks. The tide gradually turned in favor of the US Army as field artillery battalions accumulated on the heights above the towns and pummeled the German attacks. Once again, the Panther battalions were forced to engage in close-range battles, stripped of panzergrenadiers by US artillery, and vulnerable to American tank fire and bazookas in the towns. On December 26, Task Force McGeorge launched an attack to retake Grandmenil, which coincided with a push by the Panthers of the SS-Pz.Rgt. 2 out of the town. The Shermans were no match for the Panthers on open ground and lost all but two tanks. However, the skirmish halted the German attack, the high watermark for the German advance in this sector. The 116th Panzer Division had no more success to the west around Hotton, and in the days after Christmas, its attacks had stalled and losses mounted.

DUEL AT FREYNEUX: CHRISTMAS EVE, 1944

A skirmish at Freyneux helps to illustrate the disparities in combat of the Panther and M4A3 (76mm) while at the same time underlining the importance of tactical circumstances in determining the outcome of tank-versus-tank duels. The skirmish was one of many that took place in the days before and after Christmas between elements of the 3rd Armored Division and the 2nd SS-Panzer Division around Manhay. Task Force Kane was part of the widely scattered 3rd Armored Division and

The Panther Ausf. G tank's 7.5cm KwK 42 gun was aimed through a TFZ 12a (*Turmzielfernrohr*) monocular telescope in place of the binocular TZF 12 used in the Panther Ausf. D. The telescope operated at two magnifications, 2.5 and 5 power, with the lower magnification being used for general observation at which point the gunner switched to the higher magnification for precision aiming. The TZF 12a telescopic sight had an engraved reticle consisting of an aiming triangle in the center with smaller triangles on either side. The gunner placed the target at the apex of the center triangle. This reticle provided a limited stadiametric ranging capability which allowed a well-trained gunner to estimate the range based on the size of the target compared to the large triangle. The unit of measure was a graduation (*strich*) equaling 1m at 1,000m range with the larger triangle having sides of 4 graduations and the smaller triangle having sides of 2 graduations. So for example, a Sherman tank was about 2.7m wide, so if the front view of the tank filled the center triangle, it was about 670m away. Needless to say, such calculations were too difficult in the heat of battle, so a gunner had to be so well trained that the procedure became instinctive. In actual practice, the gunner's often used the co-axial machine gun to determine range. The series of triangles was intended to provide the gunner with a method to gauge the speed of a crossing target, but once again, this was too complicated to calculate during real engagements and depended on excellent training. The small graduations around the periphery of the reticle were to help adjust the weapon depending on the weapon and type of ammunition being used. The gunner would dial in either the machine gun or main gun graduations, and set the range of the ammunition type at the apex of the upper triangle, seen here set at 900m for the Pzgr 39/42 armor-piercing projectile. This would adjust the telescope relative to the gun to provide for the modest change in elevation needed to compensate for the drop of the projectile at varying ranges.

An M4 medium tank of the 4th Armored Division takes part in operations to push out of Bastogne on January 3, 1945. A .30cal machine-gun team is positioned amid the snow in the foreground. (NARA)

was deployed to the southwest of Manhay. Task Force Kane included 12 Sherman tanks and five M5A1 light tanks from the 32nd Armored Regiment, four more M5A1 light tanks of the divisional reconnaissance battalion, six M7 105mm howitzer motor carriages (HMC) of the 54th Armored Field Artillery Battalion, and an engineer squad. Their main mission was to secure the village of Dochamps to the west from the advancing 560th Volksgrenadier Division. An initial effort to seize Dochamps on the morning of December 23 was stymied by a vigorous defense by Volksgrenadier Regiment (VGR) 1129, and Task Force Kane pulled back into the neighboring villages of Lamormenil and Freyneux where it was reinforced with eight 3-in. antitank guns of the 643rd Tank Destroyer Battalion, two of which went to Freyneux. That evening,

A burned-out Panther Ausf. G of the 2nd SS-Panzer Division lies in a fork in the road between Manhay and Grandmenil after the fighting on Christmas Eve with the 3rd Armored Division. (NARA)

reinforcements in the form of the 1st Battalion, 517th Parachute Infantry of the 82nd Airborne Division arrived and were hastily sent on an ill-advised night attack against Dochamps, which was quickly repulsed. Task Force Kane spent most of December 23 resisting attacks on the two villages by VGR 1130. Defenses in Freyneux at the end of the day included two Shermans and two M5A1 light tanks covering the roads to the southwest and three Shermans and two light tanks covering the southeast. This latter force was led by 1Lt Charles Myers on an M4A3 (76mm) numbered D-31, the platoon sergeant Alvin Beckmann's M4A1 (75mm) numbered D-34, and Sgt Recce Graham's D-32, plus a pair of M5A1 light tanks of the 3rd Platoon, 83rd Reconnaissance Battalion along with about 45 dismounted reconnaissance troops.

Around dawn on December 24, VGR 1130 again attacked toward Freyneux with assault gun support but was beaten off. Following behind was a kampfgruppe of the 2nd SS-Panzer Division based around SS-PzGren.Rgt. 3 and supported by two companies of Panther tanks of I./SS-Pz.Rgt. 2. The 2. and 3./SS-Pz.Rgt. 2 were assigned to spearhead the attack, with panzergrenadiers riding the Panthers in the first wave to save fuel. The columns began moving out of Odeigne with plans to advance up the road northward to seize Oster and then move on to the main objective of Manhay. In the lead was Untersturmführer Fritz Langanke's 1st Platoon. The kampfgruppe passed to the east of Freyneux through a gap between Task Force Kane and Task Force Brewster around 0800hrs and had been informed that Freyneux was "lightly defended." Even though it was not a major objective, the kampfgruppe commander decided to send some troops to clear it, concerned that it might pose a threat to his rear during the advance on Oster and Manhay. Langanke's platoon was given the assignment, and the four Panther tanks veered off the road and headed toward the village, with the remainder of 2./SS-Pz.Rgt. 2 fording the river to the south of the bridge. Langanke spotted something on the small bridge over the Aisne River leading into the town, and fearing they were mines, headed for a river ford a short distance north, which provided access to a meadow leading into the town.

Langanke's decision to skirt the bridge put the small battle group behind the Freyneux defenses and approaching the town from the northeast. The sounds of the approaching tanks alerted the dismounted reconnaissance troops who rushed to warn the US tanks scattered through the village. Lt Myers was at an officer's briefing in the town when the Panthers appeared, so tank D-31 was commanded by the gunner, Sgt Jim Vance. Tank D-31 was near the town chapel and cemetery, partly protected by a stone wall but with a reasonably clear field of fire into the meadow north of the village. He was the first to begin engaging the Panthers as they approached. Langanke's platoon advanced in a normal skirmish line, four abreast, with Langanke in the lead at the extreme right. Vance was an experienced gunner who knew that his only chance with the 76mm gun was to hit the Panthers on the side. Since Langanke's Panther was immediately in front of his position, he engaged the other three Panthers first, beginning with one to Langanke's left. This set off an immediate ammunition fire and the crew abandoned their Panther. The panzergrenadiers abandoned the Panthers and tried to find cover. Vance then engaged the Panther on the eastern side of the platoon that had exposed its belly while moving up a slight rise in the terrain, again scoring a solid hit that set the tank on fire. Before he could engage the third tank, it was hit by another US tank but not knocked out; the Panther slowly began backing away from Freyneux. In the wake of the sudden volley of tank fire, Langanke vainly struggled to locate the enemy guns. The bright snow cover of the field contrasted sharply with the dark shape of the village and neighboring hills, and Langanke ordered his tank to a hull down position which gave him some slight protection. As he advanced, he noticed the rear end of an M4A1 D-34 that was in an ambush position facing a crossroads in the town but with the turret turned away from the meadow. Sgt Beckmann had barely arrived back on his tank and ordered the turret swung in reverse when Langanke's Panther hit it in the rear, setting it on fire. In the meantime, Langanke's tank had become the subject of every US gun in the village. His gunner tried to engage the two Shermans remaining in the village but only managed to knock down parts of the walls protecting them. After his tank had been hit on the glacis plate about ten times and the welds cracked, Langanke decided it was time to withdraw, and he ordered his Panther back behind the riverbank.

As Langanke was withdrawing, a column of Panthers from 3./SS-Pz.Rgt. 2 continued up the road for the main attack on Oster, unknowingly exposing themselves to fire from the village. Sgt Graham's D-32 had not been able to engage Langanke's Panther, which was hidden by terrain, but he saw the other Panthers at a range of about 2,000 yards. Graham could see from the tracer on his first round that he had missed, but passing corrections to the gunner, the second round impacted the side of the Panther, setting off its ammunition. A second Panther attempted to respond but was knocked out by a hit through the thin rear armor.

While the fighting was going on in the meadow, another platoon of Panthers had crossed the river to the east of the village. The 2./SS-Pz.Rgt. 2 commander, Alfred Hargesheimer, led the six Panthers toward the perimeter, spotting one of the reconnaissance battalion's M5A1 light tanks and knocking it out with two hits. The M5A1 commander, Sgt Adolfo Villanueba, escaped, ran over to one of the tanks holding the western side of the village, and directed it to an ambush position to oppose Hargesheimer's advance. The lead Panther was hit multiple times, and even though the Panther was not penetrated, the gun was jammed and the loader injured, so Hargesheimer ordered his driver to withdraw. As the other five Panthers pulled back, one more was hit and knocked out. The fighting quieted for a time as US fighter-bombers appeared and strafed the German column. The Freyneux position was reinforced by a platoon of paratroopers shortly before it was attacked by a panzergrenadier platoon, which managed to hit another M5A1 light tank with a panzerschreck antitank rocket before being pushed out of the village.

In the late afternoon, a platoon of four Shermans of Co. C, 14th Tank Battalion, 9th Armored Division were relieved from a roadblock assignment north of Freyneux and began moving across a field to the northwest of the village, completely unaware of the fighting that had been going on in the village all day. Langanke's damaged Panther was behind a depression in the riverbed, and the gunner had prudently ranged the field, using machine gun fire earlier in the day during a lull in the fighting. The Shermans advanced across the field with their weak side armored exposed, and

TANK SKIRMISH AROUND FREYNEUX, BELGIUM, DECEMBER 24, 1944

1. Panther tanks of the kampfgruppe advance up the road from Odeigne.
2. 1st Platoon, II./SS-Pz.Rgt.2 under Untersturmführer Fritz Langanke decides bridge of the Aisne River is mined.
3. Four Panther's of Langanke's platoon fords the Aisne further north, entering open meadow north of Freyneux.
4. Remaining seven Panthers under Obersturmbannführer Alfred Hargesheimer from II./SS-Pz.Rgt. 2 ford Aisne below bridge, take up positions in woods facing Freyneux.
5. Corp Vance's M4A1 (76mm) from Co. D, 32nd Armored spots advancing Panthers and begins to engage, hitting all four, but knocking out only two.
6. Two of Langanke's Panthers are penetrated and the crews bail out; his tank and another are hit.
7. Before retreating, Langanke spots an M4A1 (D-34) and knocks it out with a hit to the rear.
8. Langanke's two surviving Panthers retreat back toward the bridge and take up positions in a wooded depression.
9. Sgt Graham's M4A3 (76mm) spots III./SS-Pz. 2 on road heading toward Oster and begins firing at extreme range, knocking out two Panthers
10. After losing two Panthers plus damage to others, remainder of III./SS-Pz.Rgt. 2 withdraws into the cover of the woods.
11. The remaining Panthers of Hargesheimer's II./SS-Pz.Rgt. 2 move on the town from the east, knock out an M5A1 light tank but are beaten back by US tank fire, losing one Panther with Hargesheimer's own Panther damaged.
12. 3rd Platoon, Company C, 14th Tank Battalion, 9th Armored Division is relieved of roadblock duty in La Fosse around 1500hrs; begins moving southwest unaware of tank fighting around Freyneux and is hit by Langanke's Panther, losing four Shermans.

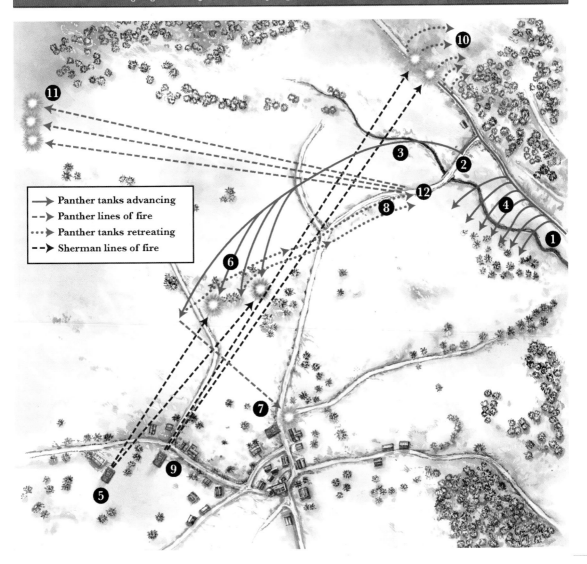

Panther tanks advancing
Panther lines of fire
Panther tanks retreating
Sherman lines of fire

On Christmas Eve, the 2. SS-Panzer Division swept through Manhay and into Grandmenil, pushing aside Task Force Kane from the 3rd Armored Division. This was one of the Das Reich Panthers lost in the fighting and is typical of the configuration of the tanks that fought at Freyneux. (NARA)

Langanke's Panther hit them in succession, knocking out all four.

By the end of the day, the battlefield was littered with burning tanks: five Panthers, five Shermans, and two M5A1 light tanks, with at least three more Panthers damaged, including those of Langanke and Hargesheimer. While the tally of tank kills was similar, the results were not. Task Force Kane had succeeded in its mission of holding the villages of Lamormenil and Freyneux, and the German attacks had failed to dislodge them or to open a gateway into Manhay from the southwest. This failure set the stage for the attack by the remaining Panther companies that night, including Barkmann's famous rampage through the US tank columns.

This skirmish helps illustrate a number of points raised earlier in this book. Nearly all of the tanks knocked out in the fighting were hit before they were even aware of the presence of enemy tanks, reaffirming the rule of "spot first, engage first, hit first." The Panther's frontal armor was a formidable defense – and the reason for Langanke and Hargesheimer's survival. Had the positions been reversed, a Sherman would certainly have been knocked out. But the Panther was not invulnerable as the fate of Langanke's platoon indicates. Even if the Panther was nearly invulnerable in a head-to-head, one-on-one encounter, in actual circumstances with multiple tanks involved across a skirmish line of a few hundred feet, enough of the Panther's side armor was exposed and vulnerable against an experienced tank crew like those of the 3rd Armored Division.

The 2nd Armored Division attacked the exposed flank of 2nd Panzer Division on Christmas. Here a group of M4A1 (76mm) carry infantry into an assault near Frandeux on December 27. (NARA)

THE RACE TO NOWHERE

The most dramatic advance in the Ardennes occurred further west in the open country beyond Bastogne. Reconnaissance elements of the 2nd Panzer Division approached within 9km of the Meuse River at Dinant on December 23, followed by the division's Panther battalion on Christmas Eve. But Allied forces were closing in from two sides with British Shermans of the 3rd Royal Tank Regiment crossing the Meuse near Dinant, engaging the reconnaissance elements of the 2nd Panzer Division. On Christmas Day, 2nd Panzer Division was hit full force by the onrushing US 2nd Armored Division, while the Panzer Lehr and 9th Panzer Divisions following behind were held at bay by the accompanying 4th Cavalry Group. Rescue attempts by the 9th Panzer Division proved futile, and the 2nd Armored Division retook Humain in costly fighting. Much of the 2nd Panzer Division was trapped near Celles, and with no prospect for rescue, the survivors were authorized to escape in small groups, abandoning their equipment. By month's end, 2nd Panzer Division was no longer combat effective. Manteuffel realized that the intervention of Collins' VII Corps had put an end to any hope of reaching the Meuse, and the offensive had obviously failed.

Patton's Third Army began moving forces toward Bastogne around midnight on December 19, covering a distance of about 150 miles. The spearhead of the advance was the 4th Armored Division, badly understrength after a month of fighting in the Saar with no time for refitting. That day it had 149 Shermans, 13 of them the M4A3 (76mm); a total of 15 percent of its tanks were dead-lined with mechanical problems, leaving a force of 127 Sherman tanks instead of the authorized 168. The first leg of the trip of over 100 miles was made in 19 hours; it was the last 16 miles that would involve four days of fighting. The lead elements

OVERLEAF

Panthers attack Freyneux, Belgium, December 24, 1944.

This scene depicts the opening stage of the attack by Langanke's Panther platoon towards Freyneux on the morning of December 24, 1944. The tanks were moving slightly downhill towards the village from a rise, with the terrain being mostly an open, snow covered meadow, interrupted here and there by a few trees. Langanke's platoon had SS panzergrenadiers riding on them, about 6–8 men per tank, prior to the first tank being hit.

63

A trio of Panther Ausf. G of Pz.Rgt. 9 lay burned out in a field outside Humain, Belgium, on December 28, 1944, after a battle with the US 2nd Armored Division on December 27. (NARA)

of the division finally reached the outskirts of Bastogne on Christmas, and the first tank entered the city on the afternoon of December 26. As the rest of the division reached the city the following day, they had 76 Shermans operational and 45 more dead-lined with mechanical problems. The newer M4A3 (76mm) held out better with none dead-lined; it was mostly the old M4 (75mm) tanks that had been in operation since August 1944 that were the source of the mechanical problems, having put on over 2,000 miles since Normandy. It was a clear reminder of the essential durability of the Sherman. As reinforcements, the 4th Armored Division in Bastogne received the first shipment of about 20 of the new M4A3E8 (76mm) with the improved suspension and wider tracks.

The Wehrmacht made a last-ditch attempt to redeem its failing offensive in the days after Christmas, rallying its forces from across the Ardennes front in a final attempt to overwhelm Bastogne. Even the remnants of 1st SS-Panzer Division were shifted from the northern shoulder to take part in the Bastogne fighting. But time had run out for the Wehrmacht, and US forces were pouring in from both the Third and Ninth Armies, giving the US Army an overwhelming advantage. Dietrich's 6th SS-Panzer Army was ordered to go on the defensive on December 27. It would take another three weeks for the US Army to erase the bulge, as much due to the appalling winter weather as German resistance.

STATISTICS AND ANALYSIS

TANK FIGHTING IN 1944: TECHNOLOGY OR TACTICS?

Tank-versus-tank fighting in autumn 1944 was not the most common type of tank combat, and contrary to the popular perception, seldom involved the clash of large numbers of tanks. The US Army's Ballistics Research Lab (BRL) conducted some operational research of tank-versus-tank fighting in an effort to determine what factors led to battlefield success. Statistical data was not regularly collected by either side during the war, so the evaluation team sifted through data from the records of the US 3rd and 4th Armored Divisions, which saw as much or more tank-versus-tank fighting as the other US divisions. In total, some 98 engagements from August through the end of December 1944 were identified and quantified, including 33 from the Ardennes fighting.

These records indicate that typical tank-versus-tank engagements were usually small unit actions, on average involving nine tanks on the US side and four Wehrmacht AFVs; less than one-third of the engagements involved more than three German AFVs. The average range at which the US tanks inflicted kills on the panzers was 893 yards, while German kills on average were from 946 yards.

The study concluded that the single most important factor in tank-versus-tank fighting was which side spotted the enemy first, engaged first, and hit first. This gave the defender a distinct advantage, since the defending tanks were typically stationary in a well-chosen ambush position. The defenders had likely avenues of approach under surveillance and ranges predetermined, which increased the accuracy of their guns. In contrast, attacking forces were generally on the move, and World War II tanks seldom fired on the move against enemy tanks due to the extremely low level of accuracy. Of the incidents studied, defenders fired first 84 percent of the time. When defenders fired first, the attackers suffered 4.3 times more casualties than the defender. When attackers fired first, the defenders suffered 3.6 times more casualties than the attackers. This see-first/hit-first advantage is a statistical correlation, not the cause of the tactical success. The side that saw first and hit first usually had an advantage in the first critical minute of the engagement since it wasn't only the first rounds fired that had such an effect, but neighboring friendly tanks also tended to fire shortly after, overwhelming the enemy force with a sudden volley of fire. Tank-versus-tank engagements tended to be short, violent affairs, with the losing side quickly withdrawing rather than face annihilation.

The study concluded that the evidence was not adequate to assess whether the technical advantage of specific tank types had any effect in the outcome of the tank engagements. This was largely a factor of the small size of the sample and the inadequate data base. During 29 engagements involving Shermans and Panthers, the Shermans had an average numerical advantage of 1.2:1. The data suggests that the Panther was 1.1 times more effective than the Sherman when fighting from the defense, while the Sherman had an 8.4 advantage against the Panther when fighting from the defense. The overall record suggests that the Sherman was 3.6 times more effective than the Panther. This ratio was probably not typical of all Sherman-versus-

SHERMAN GUNSIGHT VIEW

An approaching Panther tanks, 800 yards away. One of the major problems for gunners was the tendency of the gun to stir up dust and debris.

This is shown here with the tracer from the projectile visible slightly over the Panther. If necessary commands would be called by the commander or neighbouring tanks.

Panther exchanges during the war and may also be due to inadequate data collection. Nevertheless, the popular myths that Panthers enjoyed a 5-to-1 kill ratio against Shermans or that it took five Shermans to knock out a Panther have no basis at all in the historical records. The outcome of tank-versus-tank fighting was more often determined by the tactical situation than the technical situation. Technical advantages could be outweighed by tactical circumstances. Crew training was an important ingredient in tank engagements since an experienced commander was more apt to spot the enemy first, a well-trained crew was more apt to engage first due to better coordination, and the tank was more likely to hit the enemy first due to the gunner's superior accuracy. But in the end, a mediocre crew in a mediocre tank sitting in an ambush position had an advantage over an excellent crew in an excellent tank advancing forward.

It is interesting to note that the US Army conducted a similar study after the Korean War tank battles of 1950, where the data was more complete. This later study concluded that the see-first/hit-first rule increased the tank effectiveness by six times and that US tanks on the defense were three times as effective against enemy tanks as when on the offense. This study also had enough data to assess whether technical advantages had an impact on tank effectiveness, and concluded that the M26 was about 3.5 times more effective than the M4A3E8. This is an interesting point as the M26 Pershing was in many respects comparable to the Panther in firepower and armor protection. A direct comparison of the technical effectiveness Sherman versus Panther in World War II is difficult to make due to disparity in crew quality while the Korean comparison is free of this factor as the M26 and M4A3E8 shared identical crew quality.

The Sherman's 76mm M1A2 gun was provided with an M71D monocular telescopic sight. The view here shows an engagement at a typical range of 800 yards. Unlike the Panther, the Sherman gunner was provided with a periscopic sight as well which he would use for general observation, switching to the telescopic sight only when engaging a target. The M71D sight had only a single magnification of 5 power, and the gunner had a small switch which enabled the reticle to be illuminated in poor lighting conditions. The reticle had range gradations for the standard M62 armor piercing projectile; the performance of the M42A1 HE projectile was essentially similar at ranges under 1,000 yards. The reticle pattern was graduated in yards, so the commander estimated the range to target, included this in his firing commands, and the gunner adjusted the sight on the target accordingly. The standard commands provided by the tank commander during an engagement were as follows:

Command	Intention
Gunner	Alerts the gunner
Tank	Indicates the target type
Shot	Indicates to the loader the type of ammunition to be loaded
Traverse...right	Indicates the direction of the target relative to the barrel location
Steady On	Continues the traverse, ends the traverse when aimed at the target
Eight hundred	Indicates the estimated range in yards
Fire	Authorizes firing

In reality, this formal sequence was too time consuming, and more often than not, crews adopted their own simplified commands with a more typical command sequence being simply: "Get that tank over by the barn on the right side of the hill".

Aggravated by the failure of Ordnance to address the Panther threat, US tank units in ETO took measures into their own hands. The 12th Army Group offered this configuration as their solution to the problem, refitting an M4A3E8 with extra armor plate on the hull front and making a number of other changes such as a coaxial .50cal machine gun and an additional machine gun for the commander. (NARA)

ASSESSMENT:

OPPOSITE PAGE
An M4A3 (76mm) of the 42nd Tank Battalion, 11th Armored Division passes by an abandoned German PzKpfw IV tank along the Houffalize road outside Bastogne on January 15, 1945. The newly arrived 11th Armored Division had a half-and-half mixture of 75mm and 76mm Shermans at this time. (NARA)

The ultimate judgment on the effectiveness of World War II tanks depends on the perspective. No US tanker was happy facing a Panther in combat; no US commander would have been happy to substitute his many Sherman tanks for a much smaller number of Panther tanks. In a head-to-head duel, the Panther Ausf. G was clearly superior to the M4A3 (76mm). Technical advantage does not always translate to victory on the battlefield, and tactical considerations were often paramount. Battle in northwestern Europe in 1944–45 was not decided by the occasional tank duel, but by combined arms attacks and defensive actions. In modern warfare, weapons require a balance of mass and quality. The M4A3 (76mm) was ultimately a better weapon than the Panther since it could be fielded in adequate numbers to carry out its missions and was technically adequate to do its job. The Sherman offered a better balance of mass and quality than did the Panther. The Panther was far too complicated and expensive, and as a result, it was never able to replace the PzKpfw IV in the panzer regiments,

Panther armor plate became increasingly brittle in 1944 as supplies of key alloys disappeared. This Panther Ausf. G is from the Panzer Lehr Division, knocked out during the attacks on Buissonville after Christmas. The two hits on the front turret side caused the plate to break away in large chunks, instead of creating small holes. (NARA)

Panther Tank/Personnel status in Panther Units, Autumn 1944

Date (1944)	September 1–5		October 1		November 1		December 16		Ardennes losses*
	Panthers	Troops	Panthers	Troops	Panthers	Troops	Panthers	Troops	Panthers
Pz.Rgt. 3 (2.Pz.Div.)	3	43%	0	68%	5	67%	64	96%	20
Pz.Rgt. 33 (9.Pz.Div.)	26	76%	53	85%	45	97%	60	100%	16
Pz.Rgt.16 (116.Pz.Div.)	1	68%	28	83%	44	92%	64	96%	30
Pz.Rgt. 130 (Pz. Lehr Div.)	13	54%	0	85%	16	99%	29	95%	6
SS-Pz.Rgt. 1 (1.SS-Pz.Div.)	4	74%	3	81%	25	95%	42	100%	30
SS-Pz.Rgt. 2 (2.SS-Pz.Div.)	6	58%	1	79%	1	100%	58	100%	24
SS-Pz.Rgt. 9 (9.SS-Pz.Div.)	5	35%	19	54%	2	100%	58	124%	30
SS-Pz.Rgt.12 (12.SS-Pz.Div.)	4	29%	3	75%	23	89%	41	100%	24
Total (average percent)	62	55%	107	75%	161	92%	416	101%	180

*Does not include broken down tanks still in German hands

SHERMAN TANK STRENGTH US ARMY 12TH ARMY GROUP:

Balance of 75mm vs 76mm M4 medium tanks*					
	Sep 44	Oct 44	Nov 44	Dec 44	Jan 45
Sep. Tank Battalions					
75mm	527	508	647	525	695
76mm	95	37	166	177	259
Subtotal	622	545	813	702	954
Percent 76mm	*15.2%*	*6.7%*	*20.4%*	*25.2%*	*27.1%*
Armored Divisions					
75mm	832	719	1,041	852	955
76mm	182	202	239	423	359
Subtotal	1,014	921	1,280	1,275	1,314
Percent 76mm	*17.9%*	*21.9%*	*18.6%*	*33.1%*	*27.3%*
12th Army Group					
75mm subtotal	1,359	1,227	1,688	1,377	1,650
76mm subtotal	277	239	405	600	618
Total M4	1,636	1,466	2,093	1,977	2,268
Percent 76mm	*16.9%*	*16.3%*	*19.3%*	*30.3%*	*27.2%*

*Strength at beginning of month

and it still represented less than one-half the panzer force in December 1944. As a result, it was impossible to consider using it in German infantry divisions, which were forced to rely on less versatile assault guns. In contrast, the Sherman could be built in

To put an end to the Panther threat, the Allied air forces reinvigorated the bombing campaign against the German tank plants. The MHN plant in Hanover was shut down in March 1945 as its supplies were cut off and its assembly lines repeatedly bombed. (NARA)

	US First Army Sherman Tank Strength/Losses, Autumn 1944							
	September		October		November		December	
	Operational*	Losses	Operational	Losses	Operational	Losses	Operational	Losses
2nd AD	221	7	197	17	n/a		187	26
3rd AD	193	74	193	12	196	51	176	44
5th AD	137	20	143	10	142	3	131	48
7th AD	n/a**		117	37	n/a		102	72
9th AD	n/a		167	0	167	0	158	45
10th AD	n/a		n/a		n/a		156	7
70th TB	48	3	52	0	41	23	31	9
707th TB	54	0	52	0	43	26	40	26
709th TB	n/a		38	0	36	5	33	12
740th TB	n/a		n/a		9	0	17	5
741st TB	40	5	41	0	49	0	47	18
743rd TB	43	1	34	22	n/a		40	9
745th TB	44	7	35	17	31	5	27	5
746th TB	42	17	34	16	33	4	37	8
747th TB	40	5	45	1	47	16	n/a	
750th TB	n/a		n/a		n/a		47	7
771st TB	n/a		n/a		n/a		42	9
774st TB	n/a		53	0	52	0	49	17
Total	862	139	1,201	132	846	133	1,320	367

* Average daily operational strength
**n/a: Not assigned to First Army this month

substantially larger numbers, so that it equipped both the armored divisions and the separate tank battalions of the infantry divisions. The combat power of the infantry divisions, especially in offensive operations, was substantially enhanced by routine tank support by Sherman tank battalions. Furthermore, the US Army's insistence on durability meant that not only did the US Army have more tanks but had more tanks in action on the battle line since a smaller percentage were dead-lined with mechanical problems than was the case in Panther battalions.

At the end of two weeks of intense fighting, the Panther regiments in the Ardennes were shattered, losing about 180 tanks or 43 percent of the starting force of about 415 Panthers. Of the remaining 235 Panthers, only 45 percent were operational, and the remaining 55 percent were dead-lined with mechanical problems or battle damage. In the case of the US First Army, which bore the brunt of the Ardennes fighting, by the end of December it had lost about 320 Sherman tanks of which about 90 were M4A1/A3 (76mm), equivalent to about one-quarter of its average daily strength that month. Due to continual reinforcements, First Army had about 1,085 Shermans on hand at the end of December 1944 with about 980 operational and only 9 percent dead-lined with mechanical problems or battle damage.

CONCLUSION

Although the Panther is widely viewed as the best tank of World War II, its combat record against the US Army in the ETO in 1944–45 was often poor, especially when it was used on offensive missions. On occasion, small numbers of Panthers in the hands of battle-experienced crews inflicted disproportionate casualties on US tank units in small unit actions but not often enough to have a significant impact on the course of the war. The Panther's technological virtues could not shield it from the general decline of the Wehrmacht in 1944–45: industrial collapse leading to production shortages, poor quality control and lack of spare parts; severe shortages of

A Panther Ausf. G tank from the 9th SS-Panzer Division, knocked out near the village church in Sterpigny, Belgium, after having been hit in the rear by an M36 90mm GMC of the 703rd Tank Destroyer Battalion during fighting there in the final days of December 1944. (NARA)

This is another Panther tank knocked out in the violent fighting for Hotton in the days after Christmas 1944, with a penetration evident on the hull side. The photo shows an example of the improved Panther Ausf. G with the next deepened "chin" on the mantlet. (NARA)

fuel, which hampered training and combat operations; the declining quality of panzer crews in the later months of the war; and poor tactical decision making such as the Avranches, Lorraine, and the Ardennes operations. The Sherman was a tactical success in the ETO because it was part of a well-trained combined arms team fighting alongside determined infantry and supported by superb field artillery and ample tactical air support operating within the context of more sober tactical decision-making. Maj (Dr) P. E. Schramm, historian of the German high command, concluded that the Battle of the Bulge finally demonstrated the armored superiority of the US Army over the Wehrmacht.

The Panther disappeared from the battlefield after World War II though its influence continued to linger. The sting of the Panther's potent 75mm gun complled the Allies to field a new generation of medium tanks in the late 1940s such as the US Pershing, British Centurion and Soviet T-54. These tanks were strongly influenced by the Panther's firepower and armor protection, while at the same time they tried to avoid the Panther's automotive fragility and unsuitablity for mass production. The Battle of the Bulge marked an important turning point in tank development, raising the question whether the World War II triumvirate of light, medium, and heavy tanks was relevant any longer. The light tank had diminishing utility on the battlefield, and the new medium tanks such as the Panther and its Allied equivalents were usurping the power of the wartime heavy tanks. It can certainly be argued that the Panther was the forebearer of the modern main battle tank concept.

BIBLIOGRAPHY

This book is based in part on unpublished archival material, especially from the US Army. For example, the ETO AFV & W Section kept a daily status report of US tank strength by type and whether operational or in repair; this was used to calculate Sherman reliability rates. Likewise, the various US Army AFV & W Sections in the headquarters of the 12th Armored Group, First Army, and other formations kept strength and loss records also used to compile data presented here. Besides the printed reports of the US Strategic Bombing Survey (USSBS) listed below, I also

After nearly reaching the Meuse River, the vanguard of the 2.Panzer Division became trapped in a pocket near Celles, Belgium and overwhelmed by the US 2nd Armored Division. Here, the US Army retrieves an abandoned PzKpfw IV and Panther Ausf. G; the division's trident emblem is visible on the rear of the PzKpfw IV. (NARA)

examined the working files of the USSBS teams covering other German tank plants associated with the Panther program such as MNH and Daimler-Benz. The German perspective on the campaign is provided by the numerous Foreign Military Studies (FMS) prepared by German military officers about the Ardennes campaign. There is a very extensive collection of US Army After-Action Reports available at US National Archives and Records Administration (NARA) II, and I examined some specific units, but for reasons of space, these numerous US armored division and tank battalion histories are not listed here. The archival records were obtained primarily at the NARA at College Park, Maryland, and at the US Army Military History Institute at Carlisle Barracks, Pennsylvania, while the British reports came primarily from the Tank Museum, Bovington.

ARMY REPORTS AND STUDIES

British Army

British Intelligence Objectives Sub-Committee, Ministry of Supply, *Investigations in Germany by Tank Armament Research* (1946)

Department of Tank Design, *Preliminary Report on Armour Quality and Vulnerability of Pz.Kw. Mk V Panther*, Chobham Report M6815A/3

Fighting Vehicles Design Department, *The Transmission of the German Panther Tank*, Report No. TN 65/1 (1946)

Military Operational Research Report, *Motion Studies of German Tanks*, No. 61, Study No. 11

German Army

Generalinspekteur der Panzertruppen, *Panther-Fibel* (D655/27)

US War Department

Armored School, *Armor at Bastogne* (May 1949)

Armored School, *Armor Under Adverse Conditions: 2nd and 3rd Armored Divisions in the Ardennes Campaign* (1949)

Armored School, *2nd Armored Division in the Ardennes* (1948)

Army Ground Forces Observer Board, ETO, *Reports of Observers-ETO: 1944–45*, Volume VI (1945)

Army Concepts Analysis Agency, *Ardennes Campaign Data Base* (1995)

Ballistics Research Laboratories, *Data on WWII Tank Engagements Involving the US Third and Fourth Armored Divisions*, Memo report No. 798 (1954)

General Board, *Tank Gunnery*, Study No. 53 (1946)

HQ ETO AFV & W Section, *Daily Tank Status June 1944–May 1945*

Office of the Chief of Military History, *Tank Fight of Rocherath-Krinkelt (Belgium) 17–19 December 1944* (1952)

Office of the Chief of Military History, *Ardennes Campaign Statistics 16 December 1944–19 January 1945* (1952)

Operational Research Office, *Survey of Allied Tank Casualties in World War II*,

ORO-T-117 March (1951)

Operational Research Office, *Tank-vs.-Tank Combat in Korea*, ORO-T-278 (September 1954)

US Strategic Bombing Survey, (German) *Tank Industry Report* (1947)

US Strategic Bombing Survey, *Maschinenfabrik Augsberg-Nurnberg, Nurnberg, Germany* (1947)

US Strategic Bombing Survey, *Maybach Motor Works, Friedrichshafen, Germany* (1947)

War Department, *Medium Tank M4 (105mm Howitzer) and Medium Tank M4A1 (76mm Gun)*, TM9-731AA (June 1944)

Watertown Arsenal Lab, *Metallurgical Examination of 3¼" Thick Armor Plate from a German PzKw Panther Tank*, Report 710/715 (January 1945)

Watertown Arsenal Lab, *Metallurgical Examination of Armor and Welded Joints from the Side of German PzKw Panther Tank*, Report 710/750 (May 1945)

US Army Foreign Military Studies, Office Chief of Military History

Bayerlein, Fritz, *Panzer Lehr Divison 1 Dec 44-26 Jan 45* (A-941)

Kraas, Hugo, *12th SS Panzer Divison 15 Nov-15 Dec 1944* (B-522)

Lehmann, Rudolf, *I SS Panzer Corps-Ardennes-Special Questions* (A-926)

Peiper, Joachim, *Kampfgruppe Peiper* (C-004)

———— *I SS Panzer Corps- 15 Oct-16 Dec 1944* (B-577)

Preiss, Hermann, *Commitment of the I SS panzer Corps during the Ardennes Offensive* (A-877)

Stumpff, Horst, *Tank Maintenance in the Ardennes Offensive* (Ethint-61)

von Manteuffel, Hasso, *Fifth Panzer Army – Ardennes Offensive* (B-151, B-151a)

Wagener, Carl, *Main Reasons for the Failure of the Ardennes Offensive* (A-963)

Books

Bird, Lorrin, and Robert Livingstone, *World War II Ballistics: Armor and Gunnery*, Albany, NY, Overmatch (2001)

Cavanagh, William, *The Battle East of Elsenborn & the Twin Villages*, Barnsley, UK, Pen & Sword (2004)

De Meyer, Stephan, et. al., *Duel in the Mist: The Leibstandardte During the Ardennes Offensive*, Vol. 1, AFV Publications (2007)

Dugdale, J., *Panzer Divisions, Panzer Grenadier Divisons, Panzer Brigades of the Army and Waffen SS in the West: Ardennes and Nordwind, Their Detailed and Precise Strengths and Organizations (Vol I, Part 1: September 1944; Part 2: October 1944; Part 3: November 1944, Part 4A, 4B, 4C: December 1944)*, Military Press, Buckinghamshire, UK (2000–2005)

Hahn, Fritz, *Waffen und Geheimwaffen des deutschen Heeres 1933–45, Band 2: Panzer und Sonderfahrzeuge, Wunderwaffen, Verbrauch und Verluste*, Berard & Graefe, Berlin (1987)

Hubert Meyer, *The History of the 12.SS-Panzerdivison Hitlerjugend*, Fedrowicz,

Winnipeg, Manitoba (1994)

Jentz, Thomas, *Germany's Panther Tank: The Quest for Combat Supremacy*, Schiffer, Atglen, PA (1995)

Spielberger, Walter, *Panther and its Variants*, Schiffer, Atglen, PA (1993)

Tiemann, Ralf, *The Leibstandarte Volume IV/2*, Fedorowicz, Winnipeg, Manitoba (1998)

Vannoy, Allyn, and Jay Karamales, A*gainst the Panzers: US Infantry vs. German Tanks 1944–45*, McFarland, Jefferson, NC (1996)

Winter, George, *Freineux and Lamormenil-The Ardennes*, Fedorowicz, Winnipeg, Manitoba (1990)

——————— *Manhay, The Ardennes: Christmas 1944*, Fedorowicz, Winnipeg, Manitoba (1990)

INDEX

Figures in **bold** refer to illustrations.